Gerald R. Ford

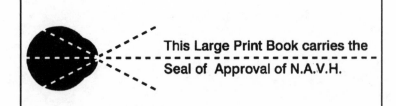

This Large Print Book carries the
Seal of Approval of N.A.V.H.

THE AMERICAN PRESIDENTS

GERALD R. FORD

DOUGLAS BRINKLEY

ARTHUR M. SCHLESINGER, JR.,
GENERAL EDITOR

THORNDIKE PRESS

An imprint of Thomson Gale, a part of The Thomson Corporation

Detroit • New York • San Francisco • New Haven, Conn. • Waterville, Maine • London

LIBRARY OF CONGRESS CATALOGING-IN-PUBLICATION DATA

Brinkley, Douglas.
   Gerald R. Ford / Douglas Brinkley.
     p. cm. — (The American presidents)
   Includes bibliographical references and index.
   ISBN-13: 978-0-7862-9728-3 (lg. print : hardcover : alk. paper)
   ISBN-10: 0-7862-9728-X (lg. print : hardcover : alk. paper)
   1. Ford, Gerald R., 1913–2006. 2. Presidents — United States —
Biography. 3. United States — Politics and government — 1974–1977. I.
Title.
   E866.B75 2007b
   973.925092—dc22
   [B]   2007013787

Published in 2007 by arrangement with Henry Holt and Company LLC.

Printed in the United States of America on permanent paper
10 9 8 7 6 5 4 3 2 1

For my mother and father,
who brought me to hear
Gerald Ford speak
in Bowling Green, Ohio,
when I was eleven years old

CONTENTS

EDITOR'S NOTE 9

1. Michigan Upbringing 15
2. Man of the House. 38
3. Foot Soldier for Nixon 66
4. The Watergate Blues 84
5. Changing of the Guard 105
6. The Pardon Meets Whip
   Inflation Now 123
7. The Agony of Peace. 153
8. The *Mayaguez* Incident and the
   Helsinki Accords 184
9. Looking for Traction 209
10. The Bicentennial Campaign . . . 244
11. Retirement Decades 274

NOTES. 295
MILESTONES 327
SELECTED BIBLIOGRAPHY. . . 343
ACKNOWLEDGMENTS 351

EDITOR'S NOTE

THE AMERICAN PRESIDENCY

The president is the central player in the American political order. That would seem to contradict the intentions of the Founding Fathers. Remembering the horrid example of the British monarchy, they invented a separation of powers in order, as Justice Brandeis later put it, "to preclude the exercise of arbitrary power." Accordingly, they divided the government into three allegedly equal and coordinate branches — the executive, the legislative, and the judiciary.

But a system based on the tripartite separation of powers has an inherent tendency toward inertia and stalemate. One of the three branches must take the initiative if the system is to move. The executive branch alone is structurally capable of taking that initiative. The Founders must have sensed this when they accepted Alexander Hamilton's proposition in the Seventieth Federalist that "energy in the executive is a leading character in the definition of good government." They thus envisaged a strong president — but within an equally strong system of constitutional accountability. (The term *imperial presidency* arose in the 1970s to describe the situation when the balance between power and accountability is upset in favor of the executive.)

The American system of self-government thus comes to focus in the presidency — "the vital place of action in the system," as Woodrow Wilson put it. Henry Adams, himself the great-grandson and grandson of presidents as well as the most brilliant of American historians, said that the American president "resembles the commander of a ship at sea. He must have a helm to grasp, a course to steer, a port to seek." The men in the White House (thus far only men, alas) in steering their chosen courses have shaped our destiny as a nation.

Biography offers an easy education in American history, rendering the past more human, more vivid, more intimate, more accessible, more connected to ourselves. Biography reminds us that presidents are not supermen. They are human beings too, worrying about decisions, attending to wives and children, juggling balls in the air, and putting on their pants one leg at a time. Indeed, as Emerson contended, "There is properly no history; only biography."

Presidents serve us as inspirations, and they also serve us as warnings. They provide bad examples as well as good. The nation, the Supreme Court has said, has "no right to expect that it will always have wise and humane rulers, sincerely attached to the principles of the Constitution. Wicked men, ambitious of power, with hatred of liberty and contempt of law, may fill the place once occupied by Washington and Lincoln."

The men in the White House express the ideals and the values, the frailties and the flaws, of the voters who send them there. It is altogether natural that we should want to know more about the virtues and the vices of the fellows we have elected to govern us. As we know more about them, we will know more about ourselves. The French political philosopher Joseph de Maistre said, "Every nation has the government it deserves."

At the start of the twenty-first century, forty-two men have made it to the Oval Office. (George W. Bush is counted our forty-third president, because Grover Cleveland, who served nonconsecutive terms, is counted twice.) Of the parade of presidents, a dozen or so lead the polls periodically conducted by historians and political scientists. What makes a great president?

Great presidents possess, or are possessed by, a vision of an ideal America. Their passion, as they grasp the helm, is to set the ship of state on the right course toward the port they seek. Great presidents also have a deep psychic connection with the needs, anxieties, dreams of people. "I do not believe," said Wilson, "that any man can lead who does not act . . . under the impulse of a profound sympathy with those whom he leads — a sympathy which is insight — an insight which is of the heart rather than of the intellect."

"All of our great presidents," said Franklin D. Roosevelt, "were leaders of thought at a time when certain ideas in the life of the nation had to be clarified." So Washington incarnated the idea of federal union, Jefferson and Jackson the idea of democracy, Lincoln union and freedom, Cleveland rugged honesty. Theodore Roosevelt and Wilson, said FDR, were both "moral leaders, each in his own way and his own time, who used the presidency as a pulpit."

To succeed, presidents not only must have a port to seek but they must convince Congress and the electorate that it is a port worth seeking. Politics in a democracy is ultimately an educational process, an adventure in persuasion and consent. Every president stands in Theodore Roosevelt's bully pulpit.

The greatest presidents in the scholars' rankings, Washington, Lincoln, and Franklin Roosevelt, were leaders who confronted and overcame the republic's greatest crises. Crisis widens presidential opportunities for bold and imaginative action. But it does not guarantee presidential greatness. The crisis of secession did not spur Buchanan or the crisis of depression spur Hoover to creative leadership. Their inadequacies in the face of crisis allowed Lincoln and the second Roosevelt to show the difference individuals make to history. Still, even in the absence of first-order crisis, forceful and persuasive presidents — Jefferson, Jackson, James K. Polk, Theodore Roosevelt, Harry Truman, John F. Kennedy, Ronald Reagan, George W. Bush — are able to impose their own priorities on the country.

The diverse drama of the presidency offers a fascinating set of tales. Biographies of American presidents constitute a chronicle of wisdom and folly, nobility and pettiness, courage and cunning, forthrightness and deceit, quarrel and consensus. The turmoil

13

perennially swirling around the White House illuminates the heart of the American democracy.

It is the aim of the American Presidents series to present the grand panorama of our chief executives in volumes compact enough for the busy reader, lucid enough for the student, authoritative enough for the scholar. Each volume offers a distillation of character and career. I hope that these lives will give readers some understanding of the pitfalls and potentialities of the presidency and also of the responsibilities of citizenship. Truman's famous sign — "The buck stops here" — tells only half the story. Citizens cannot escape the ultimate responsibility. It is in the voting booth, not on the presidential desk, that the buck finally stops.

— Arthur M. Schlesinger, Jr.

1
MICHIGAN
UPBRINGING

The executives at Harper & Row, Publishers were smart back in 1979 when they chose a black-and-white photograph of a relaxed Gerald Ford to adorn the cover of his memoir, *A Time to Heal.* Surrounding Ford were wisps of smoke from his trademark pipe, creating an ethereal aura around him. You could almost hear him go puff-puff-puff between sentences. The profile of his wide forehead and prominent jaw exuded vigor while his broad shoulders reminded everybody of his football years at the University of Michigan. The photograph, in fact, conveyed an inner steadiness of purpose, his low-key demeanor offering up an oddly calming sensation for an all-powerful commander in chief. But that, in a nutshell, was the genius of Ford. His decency was palpable. Following the traumas of the Vietnam War and Watergate, he was a tonic to the consciousness of his times, a

Middle American at ease with himself and the enduring values of our Constitution. "Nobody really knows that my real birth-name wasn't Ford," the thirty-eighth president recalled. "People think of me as a brand name for even-keeledness. But I had plenty of adversity growing up. I just chose to accentuate the positive."[1]

When Gerald Ford came into the world on July 14, 1913, in an ornate Victorian house on Woolworth Avenue in Omaha, Nebraska, he was named Leslie Lynch King Jr.[2] His mother, the former Dorothy Ayer Gardner, had been a nineteen-year-old college student when she met and soon married the well-to-do Leslie King Sr. the previous year. Her infatuation faded fast: she later charged that King punched her at the least provocation. When he flew into another violent rage two weeks after she bore their son, brandishing a knife and threatening to kill both her and the baby, Dorothy packed up her belongings and her son and fled Omaha in the cold glare of an afternoon. That she did so in an era of mores that favored spousal battery over divorce bespeaks the steel in the stock behind Jerry Ford.

Baby in tow, Dorothy moved back to her parents' house in Grand Rapids, Michigan.

Comfortably prosperous thanks to its well-regarded furniture manufacturing industry, the state's second-largest city was "one of those exceedingly agreeable, homelike American cities," with rows of neat houses tucked amid rolling hills of surrounding farmland.[3] But Grand Rapids was also decidedly unsophisticated, lacking large-scale municipal projects or much in the way of cultural activity. Relatively recent Dutch immigrants accounted for about half the local population; another quarter claimed Polish descent. The area's progress was fueled largely by these newcomers eager to work hard for a share in the American dream.

Among the city's residents was a descendant of early English settlers with a locally renowned surname. However, twenty-five-year-old Gerald Rudolf Ford was not related to the pioneering automaker Henry Ford, Michigan's leading citizen. Ford was a paint salesman with little money and less education, having dropped out of the tenth grade, but he boasted all the bedrock virtues, including honesty, charity, and a deep-seated work ethic. Dorothy Gardner King recognized his merits immediately upon meeting him at an Episcopalian church social. Ford returned her interest. He was not put off by her status as a young divorcée with a son. The couple married on February 1, 1917, and settled into a loving home.

Ford, however, never took out adoption papers for his stepson. Dorothy thought adoption would lessen her chances to procure child support from King. The couple did informally rename the child Gerald Rudolf Ford Jr. (His name would be legally changed on December 3, 1935, with the son choosing to spell his middle name "Rudolph" to give it a less Germanic cast.)[4] The elder Fords told their son he had a different biological father when he was twelve or thirteen. But when Leslie L. King Sr. approached Jerry at Bill Skougis's hamburger joint, located across from the high school, where the teen worked part-time after school, and told him he was his real father, Jerry was stunned.[5] Although Jerry accepted King's invitation to lunch, the encounter left him bitter at his birth father's long absence and resentful of his apparent wealth. King, whose own father's holdings included several businesses, land, and railroad stock, let out that he had come to Michigan from Wyoming to pick up a new Lincoln, detouring from Detroit to Grand Rapids on a whim to look up his abandoned son.[6]

The revelation of his true paternity made

little impact, however, on the boy's relationship with Gerald R. Ford Sr. Even at seventeen, the strapping youth had the good sense to recognize the firm but kind man who had raised him as his "real" dad. He admired the way his adoptive father plodded tirelessly through every detail of his business, always forgoing the quick buck in favor of steady progress toward measured financial success. He and Dorothy also devoted considerable time and effort to charitable undertakings. Among many such endeavors, the couple helped establish a community center in one of the city's racially mixed, most disadvantaged neighborhoods.

Western Michigan was a resource-rich area, and young Jerry Ford grew up seeing pine logs floating down the Grand River and wooden furniture being loaded onto trains. When Grand Rapids celebrated its centennial in 1926 the city had plenty to be proud of — a first-rate public school system, a bustling railroad depot, regular air service to Detroit, four huge movie theaters, hundreds of grocery stores, five golf courses, a low tax rate, a church on practically every city block, and a ranking as the number-one tree city in America. Virtually every lawn was manicured, and homes displayed the

Stars and Stripes year-round. Visitors came to Grand Rapids for conventions and reunions, often filling all eight thousand hotel rooms to capacity.[7]

By the late 1920s, the Ford household included four sons. Jerry and his half brothers divided their time among schoolwork, chores, and family fun. Because Michigan was blessed with blue lakes and pristine forests, many hours were spent outdoors. Early in the autumn of 1929 Gerald Ford Sr. founded the Ford Paint & Varnish Company with a partner and moved his brood into a big new house on Lake Drive in prosperous East Grand Rapids. The stock-market crash that October decimated his new venture and drained his family's carefully kept savings. The Fords left their fine new house for cheaper quarters. A Dreiserian grimness now entered the Ford household as they struggled to avoid debt. But during the Great Depression no one in the Ford family ever went to bed hungry — a tribute to the probity of Dorothy and Gerald Ford Sr. and their sons.

In the first half of the twentieth century, Michigan was largely a Republican state. In Grand Rapids, most folks seemed to accept that they had been born into the GOP fold, and just stayed there. Long before Gerald

Ford Jr. was old enough to understand the positions or even recognize the leaders of America's two main political parties, he considered himself a diehard Republican. When Ford was growing up, Michigan's leading political lights were its two U.S. senators, James Couzens and Arthur H. Vandenberg (from Grand Rapids) — both Republicans, naturally. Couzens, who had made a spectacular fortune as a founding partner in the Ford Motor Company, was irascible and politically independent. The consequences of Couzens's deviation from the party by supporting Roosevelt's New Deal programs were avidly discussed in the Ford household, along with many other civic matters that held lasting lessons for young Jerry.

In high school Jerry Ford was a good, but not too good, student; well-liked by his peers, Ford couldn't turn his charm on — or off. The sturdy, blond youth's agreeability arose from his instinct to offer, in George Bernard Shaw's phrase, "the same manner to all human souls." He was an uncomplicated teenager: a straight-arrow Eagle Scout and football star more interested in cars than girls. "Everybody had more good things about them than bad things," Ford once told a classmate. "If you accentuate the good things in dealing with a person, you can like him even though he or she had some bad qualities. If you have that attitude, you never hate anybody."[8]

Many of the highs of Jerry Ford's young life came on the football field. He excelled at center on offense and as a linebacker on defense for his South High School team. His senior year — 1930 — they took the state championship, and Jerry was named to both the all-city and all-state squads. Ford was big, but deceptively quick — just as he would prove later in the political arena. What Ford learned from football, moreover, would focus his career in public service. The frequent football analogies in his remarks revealed a political strategy of approaching every challenge — be it votes to be won or seats in the House of Representatives to be picked up — the way a good coach looks at the yards to be gained to get to each first down and over the goal line. Discipline, preparation, teamwork, and adherence to a game plan may be the platitudes of the locker room but Ford carried them onto the political field. In fact, he used them to turn the Republican Party around in the 1960s, when he led the GOP team in the House to a winning cohesion that would stand the test of time. "You play to win," he told the University of Michigan football squad in 1976 while running for president, "and that's the only way I know to move ahead, whether you are on the gridiron or whether you are in classrooms or whether you are in politics or anything else."[9]

Football also opened a world of possibilities. Although his exploits on the field won invitations for Ford to visit Harvard, Northwestern, and Michigan State, it was a group of University of Michigan alumni from his hometown who secured his education with a scholarship to play for their school. The Michigan football coach, Harry Kipke, found the prize recruit a part-time cafeteria job at Ann Arbor's University Hospital to help Ford scrimp through college in the Depression years.[10] The Wolverines went undefeated and took the Big Ten championships in both 1932 and 1933, with Jerry Ford cheering his teammates on from the bench. When most of the school's starting roster graduated, Ford finally made the first string as a senior, and was named his team's Most Valuable Player in 1934. Unfortunately, the star-depleted Wolverines lost seven of their eight games that season.

The exception came in Michigan's racially charged contest that year against Georgia

Tech, which had announced that its team would refuse to take the field with the Wolverines' Willis F. Ward, on the grounds that the star receiver was African-American. After Michigan's administrators agreed to the outrageous demand, Ford nearly took himself out of the game in protest, but decided that to do so would hurt his team even more. So on game day, when "one of the Georgia Tech linemen made the mistake of taunting the Michigan squad over its missing 'nigger' " — as Ford's press secretary Jerald F. terHorst would write decades later — "Ford and a Michigan guard blocked the lineman so savagely a few plays later that he had to be carried from the field on a stretcher."[11] The Wolverines won, 9 to 2.

Ford's senior-year MVP award earned him a starting slot in the annual East–West Shrine Game in San Francisco on New Year's Day 1935, and eight months later an even more coveted spot in the College All-Star Game against the Chicago Bears at Soldier Field. The Bears won the latter contest, 5 to 0, but Ford played well enough to elicit offers from the Green Bay Packers and the Detroit Lions, each of which dangled two hundred dollars a game for the coming fourteen-game season.[12] However, in an era when becoming a professional athlete was neither a meal ticket nor a key to later success, Jerry Ford had a solid enough academic record to turn these offers down. "It was hard to walk away from the NFL," Ford recalled. "But my ambition was to go to law school. Sometimes I'd daydream about how my life would have turned out differently if I had said 'yes' to the Lions or Packers."[13]

After graduating with a B average and a major in economics and political science in 1935, Ford moved east and became boxing coach and assistant football coach at Yale University while trying to get into law school there. Yale's officials finally relented in 1938. Even as he continued to coach, Ford swiftly proved them right to have given him a shot. Professor Eugene Rostow, a former undersecretary of state who was on Yale's law school faculty at the time, later recalled Ford as "a very solid, straightforward, decent sort of bird of moderate ability. He worked hard, did reasonably well."[14] In fact, Ford earned his LLB in 1941 with grades that put him in the top third of his class. He got his highest mark at Yale in the legal ethics course.

While at Yale, Ford fell under the spell of the America First crowd, influenced by such contemporaries as Kingman Brewster, Potter Stewart, and Sargent Shriver. Ford adopted their essentially isolationist vision; still, by all accounts he was open-minded and void of ideological certitude. It would be World War II that transformed him into an internationalist.

Ford expanded his horizons in other directions while at law school. A fairly serious relationship with an aspiring model named Phyllis Brown turned into a thousand-dollar investment in a fledgling New York agency, which led to the football star's posing in ski togs next to his girlfriend — in seventeen photographs splashed across five pages of the March 1940 issue of *Look* magazine. Ford's modeling career would end with the relationship in 1942, shortly after the couple appeared on a flag-waving *Cosmopolitan* cover. On another visit with his girlfriend in New York City early in 1940, Ford heard Republican presidential candidate Wendell Willkie speak at a rally. Willkie, a successful Wall Street financier originally from Indiana, was rumpled, rational, robust, and a political outsider aggressively averse to harsh ideologies. He immediately appealed to the innately moderate Ford. Under Willkie's influence, Ford began to abandon his collegiate flirtation with isolationism in favor of the internationalist view, which espoused planting a firm U.S. foothold on the world stage. Ford actively aligned himself with Willkie's good-government stance against the prevailing party-boss patronage system of the day. Ironically, on his father's advice Ford set out on his own crusade against that system by calling on western Michigan's GOP power broker, Frank D. McKay.

From posh offices in an eponymous building that was then the tallest in Grand Rapids, McKay ruled a political fiefdom built on real estate, banking, and insurance. He exerted an iron-fisted control over virtually every patronage job at every level of government in Michigan's Fifth District and beyond, plus the bulk of the state's juiciest public contracts. Although he called himself "a businessman first and a politician second," McKay was the man to see about working for a Republican presidential candidate in Michigan. "I thought, here I was, offering myself as a volunteer, that he would welcome me gladly, especially in my own hometown," Ford reminisced later. "Well, he made me wait outside his office for four hours and, boy, was I mad. Finally he saw me, gave me three minutes, and good-bye. Nothing."[15]

Ford took McKay's rude reception personally, as political novices will. The unusual upshot would come later, when Ford would turn his wounded dignity toward a righteous quest to oust the egotist who had dared to brush him off. Late that July, however, Ford just watched and learned from the doings at the Republican National Convention in Philadelphia. Willkie's chance at the nomination seemed to be fading as the delegate count stayed stalled after a sixth ballot. The continuing deadlock looked likely to hand the contest to Senator Robert Taft of Ohio. At that moment McKay offered to throw his support to Willkie — just when the reformist candidate needed it too desperately to turn him down. Willkie had no choice but to agree that, should he win, McKay could have undisputed sway over every patronage job in Michigan — not just the Fifth District. The price was high, but Wendell Willkie, the establishment outsider who had made a career of denouncing political bossism, shook the hand of Frank McKay and wrapped up the GOP presidential nomination on the next ballot.

The lessons Jerry Ford learned about politics that summer left an acrid aftertaste in his throat. He grew determined to topple the McKay machine. After passing the state bar exam and setting up a law partnership in Grand Rapids with Philip Buchen, a fraternity brother from the University of Michigan, Ford began meeting with other Republicans avid to overturn the status quo in western Michigan politics. The odds of a handful of amateurs dismantling such a tightly tuned machine grew even longer once the United States entered World War II. So many of the younger reformers in Ford's loose-knit alliance signed up for the service after the Japanese attack on Pearl Harbor on December 7, 1941, that the few left behind dubbed themselves the "Home Front" against McKay and all he stood for.

Ford was among those who deferred their political battles to take on the Axis powers. He joined the U.S. Naval Reserve on April 20, 1942, received his commission as an ensign and indoctrination at Annapolis, then reported as ordered to a navy preflight physical training unit headed by onetime heavyweight boxing champion Gene Tunney. Comfortably based at the University of North Carolina at Chapel Hill, the new so-called physical-fitness specialist impressed the importance of conditioning upon the recruits. Some young officers in the same cushy position might have counted their lucky stars and kept quiet, but Jerry Ford wanted to see action. Yearning for sea duty, he was finally transferred to Norfolk, Virginia, for gunnery training and then ordered to report to the just-commissioned light aircraft carrier USS *Monterey.* The strange-looking carrier had a 622-foot flight deck ensconced on top of a cruiser hull surrounded by forty antiaircraft deck guns.

Lieutenant Ford's primary duties were to oversee the antiaircraft gun crew on the fantail deck and to serve as the ship's director of physical training. The enlisted men loved him for constructing a basketball court on the hangar deck. But he also took intense interest in his later secondary role as assistant navigation officer. In October 1943 the *Monterey* headed out from San Diego to join Admiral William "Bull" Halsey's Third Fleet for some of World War II's most storied South Pacific naval operations. On November 19, planes from the *Monterey* bombed Japanese troops at Gilbert Island for nearly a month. The combat moments wouldn't cease. The *Monterey,* in fact, sank a Japanese cruiser and destroyer, with Ford directing the ship's forty-millimeter guns.

Worse than the Japanese, however, was the hellacious weather the crew encountered. When Typhoon Cobra hit the fleet off the Philippines in December 1944, more than eight hundred sailors were lost, including six from the *Monterey;* Lieutenant Ford narrowly escaped being washed overboard in the sixty-knot winds. Slipping a gas mask over his face, Ford worked tirelessly with his bucket brigade to extinguish numerous fires.[16] The ship itself sustained extensive damage and was put in dry dock for repairs. "Battered and spent," the navy declared as it mothballed the *Monterey,* "unfit for service."[17]

Ford spent the rest of the war on land, but his service record (ten battle stars) proved solid enough to earn him a promotion to the reserve rank of lieutenant commander before he was discharged from active duty in February 1946.

While in the Pacific theater, Ford had devoted some of his spare time tracking the progress of the Home Front back in Grand Rapids. In 1944, Buchen — kept out of the war by a polio-related disability — reported that the group's leaders believed they had a shot at wresting control of the Kent County Republican Party from the McKay machine. To make their bid stick, they needed a popular, respected, squeaky-clean pillar of the community to put forward for county chairman. In his son's absence, Gerald R. Ford Sr. leaped to mind on all counts; he

31

not only supported the Home Front efforts but also was head of the county's Office of Civil Defense. But the elder Ford rejected the offer.

The following Sunday, W. B. VerMeulen, the septuagenarian dentist who had formed Grand Rapids's Home Front out of loathing for everything Frank McKay represented, got a call from Gerald Ford Sr. "He said he had just come home from church and there was a special delivery letter from Jerry in the Pacific," VerMeulen recounted. Ford read parts of his son's letter aloud over the phone. "Dad," Jerry wrote, "if the Home Front ever asks you to do something, don't turn them down. I'm going to get into this thing when I get back from service and I'll take your place. So don't turn them down." Then Ford told VerMeulen that he would stand for GOP county chairman.[18]

The Home Fronters' successful installation of Gerald Ford Sr. as Kent County's Republican chairman barely put a dent in McKay's machine, although the boss's clout in the statehouse had already been softening under a spate of grand jury indictments for various forms of corruption. And McKay still had a mouthpiece in Washington: Congressman Bartel J. Jonkman. Like Senator Vandenberg and young Jerry Ford, Jonkman had started out as an isolationist firmly opposed to any U.S. involvement in foreign affairs, but unlike them had stayed so minded despite global events. Jonkman backed the war effort, of course, but he also advocated the immediate withdrawal of American troops — and, more to the point, American dollars — from faraway endeavors as soon as the fighting ended. Jonkman voted against the Marshall Plan and other recovery programs, while Senator Vandenberg sided with the internationalist position of the Truman administration.

Far from a populist, Bartel Jonkman spent most of his time in Washington toiling away at legislative and political matters while virtually ignoring his constituents back home. He seemed to consider his seat safe, relying on the backing of the McKay machine and the boost of Dutch ethnic pride. But the Home Front had other ideas in 1948. The group had an ex–University of Michigan center to push them through McKay's line.

Upon his return to Grand Rapids, Jerry Ford had rejoined his former law partner Philip Buchen at a larger, well-regarded local firm. When not practicing law or working on his golf game at the Kent Country Club, Ford began to attract some notice for his work as a veterans' advocate. He formed a vigorous association devoted to developing nice, affordable housing fast enough to accommodate all the returning servicemen struggling to rebuild civilian lives back home. Bolstered by the contempt his colleagues and the Home Front expressed for their congressman, Ford found himself drawn into action by Jonkman's aggressive isolationism, a position his own wartime experiences had convinced him was wrong. So, on June 17, 1948, Ford announced his candidacy in the Fifth District's Republican primary. Positioned as a dark horse, Ford attacked the campaign with everything he had. He assembled a highly motivated team of fellow Home Fronters around him, firmed up his positions, and worked up new game plans for promoting himself. In his own nice, approachable, effective way, Gerald Ford made friends, including some in powerful places, one by one on his way toward his goal.

Few observers gave the neophyte Ford much of a shot against McKay's venerable political machine. The most notable vote of confidence in the challenger came from Senator Vandenberg, who met Ford in private to proffer his hearty encouragement. Ford's conversion to the internationalist view fell right in line with the popular senator's — and Ford was bright enough to recognize that the reason for Vandenberg's popularity was the senator's astute grasp of what Michigan's voters wanted. Vandenberg couldn't endorse Ford, or even encourage him in public, he explained; seeing how Ford couldn't possibly win the primary, the senator would still have to live with Jonkman after the general election. (The state's Democrats were so weak that a primary victory for a Republican was virtually the same as election.) Yet even Vandenberg's whispered support would have a quiet bearing on the Fifth District race. And the senator could see that the young man's tireless campaigning would have some impact on Grand Rapids's voters.

For Jerry Ford was not only young but acted like it. He appeared anywhere and everywhere to shake hands and seduce votes. Jonkman, by contrast, made only cursory campaign visits to his home district. While few prospective voters might have called Jerry Ford charismatic, most readily acknowledged that at least he didn't seem phony. In truth, Ford had developed a stump style he found comfortable. He combined his athlete's backslapping bonhomie with simple, nice-guy good manners.

He spoke pretty well but, more important, he listened brilliantly, offering his full attention to any voter who took the time to address him.

The conventional wisdom took a pounding in Michigan's Fifth District that September. Ford not only won the Republican primary, he whipped Bartel Jonkman by 23,632 votes to 14,341.[19] Thus began a political career that would suffer only a single defeat through the next thirty years. Not once in his thirteen congressional elections did Ford take less than 60 percent of the vote, and after 1948 he never faced another primary opponent.

Ford's personal life took off in 1948 as well. On October 15, two and a half weeks before the general election that was sure to put him in the United States Congress, Gerald R. Ford Jr. married Elizabeth Ann Bloomer Warren, a vivacious young divorcée who worked as a fashion coordinator at a large Grand Rapids department store. Like her new husband, Betty Ford had spent a few years under the bright lights of New York City, doing some modeling as well as a two-year stint dancing with the renowned Martha Graham Dance Company. Worldly, bright, and fun, the new Mrs. Ford was also astute, candid, and graced with a sly sense of humor. By 1957 the couple would have four children: Michael, John, Steven, and Susan. "Betty just lit me up," Ford later said. "She touched me in a way no other woman ever could. She made me laugh and also feel protective of her."[20]

On the political front, his assiduous constituent service, knack for campaigning, and moderate record on the day's issues practically guaranteed Jerry Ford a long career in Congress. Complacency, however, was not in his character. Deceptively ambitious, from the very first Ford sought to grasp the priorities, proclivities, and pitfalls of the U.S. House of Representatives. He devised a game plan, and in his doggedly determined way he would punch it through, vote by vote, toward his goal of changing Congress as well as his party's place within it.

2
MAN OF THE HOUSE

Gerald R. Ford arrived in Washington, D.C., over the New Year holiday weekend. Eager to clean out and set up his office, Ford and his administrative aide, John P. Milanowski, showed up at the House Office Building in overalls. When a Capitol policeman barred the scruffy pair from entering the near-deserted building, Milanowski piped up, " 'S all right, Officer. He's the new congressman from Grand Rapids. I'm his assistant."[1]

Sandy-haired and still lineman-solid at thirty-five, with his unhurried Midwestern manners, Gerald Ford seemed a bit unsophisticated for the nation's capital when he took his seat in Congress on January 3, 1949. But the earnestness in his approach was simply part of the man. For all his time at Yale, his exposure to the New York fashion world, and his four years in the U.S. Navy, Ford still had the down-home air of his

Michigan origins. He may even have culti-
vated it — if acting the Rotarian meant taking nothing for granted, claiming no greater
knowledge than he actually possessed, and
seeking the counsel of his elders.

In truth, Ford was at least as ambitious as
any of his new peers in the Eighty-first
Congress, but quietly so. Behind his
humble, nice-guy demeanor — which had
the advantage of being as genuine as it was
appealing — he held a no-nonsense, busi-
nesslike view of the future and his optimal
position therein. His first congressional aide
recalled that Ford had designs on the House
leadership from the start. "We talked about
how nice it would be for Jerry to be Speaker
someday," Milanowski said. "That's where
all the patronage was, the power."[2] The
Speaker of the House of Representatives, as
leader of the majority party, oversees debates, shepherds through legislation, sways
committee appointments, and stands second
in line to succeed the president of the
United States, if need be.

Several of Ford's fellow congressmen during his early years in the House openly
coveted the White House. One of them,
Massachusetts Democrat John F. Kennedy,
occupied the suite across the corridor from
Ford's in the House Office Building. "The

net result was, Jack Kennedy and I became good friends because we walked back and forth from our offices to the House chamber when the House bell rang," Ford recalled decades later. "Our staffs became very close. We were pals. I was not familiar with his health problems, but I had many suspicions about his philandering. That was none of my business."[3] Another ambitious colleague made a point of introducing himself right after Ford had taken his first oath of office. "I'm Dick Nixon, from California," he began with extended hand. "I heard about your big win in Michigan, and I wanted to say hello and welcome you to the House."[4] The two young Republican navy vets soon became friends, and — more significant — political allies. They would stay close for life. "Incidentally, if I had been a sportswriter during the time you played center for Michigan," Nixon wrote Ford in 1994, just months before his death, "you would have been on my All-American football team."[5]

Years later, when discussing his early congressional career, Ford recalled two indelible visual memories: sitting in the House chamber hearing General Douglas MacArthur deliver his "Old Soldiers Never Die" valedictory and watching Richard Nixon zealously investigate Alger Hiss for treason on the House Un-American Activities Committee. "Both moments stayed with me in a very real sense for very real reasons," Ford recalled. "General MacArthur, after all, had led our efforts in the Pacific where I served during World War II. And Dick Nixon was my close friend and there he was creating a national ruckus by prosecuting Hiss. In MacArthur's case I was impressed by the power of oratory. In Dick's case it was more the power of dogged diligence."[6]

It didn't take Ford long to learn that Nixon was a foreign policy wizard. "We had a shared vision about the Soviet Union," Ford recalled. "But Nixon could actually tell you about all the political parties in any country. He was that micro." Ford truly respected Nixon's acumen. Both Republicans enthusiastically endorsed the Marshall Plan and U.S. military intervention on the Korean peninsula. "Our political views on global issues were nearly identical," Ford recalled. "I even agreed with him on Hiss. Domestically we were almost mirror images."[7] Something else, however, bonded them even more. Both men had gone through the Great Depression on the slum side of the socioeconomic tracks. "We understood what it meant to rise on merit, not privilege," Ford recalled. "We had a mutual love of football which really sealed the deal of our friendship. . . . Our personalities [however] were different. I tried to stay optimistic. Dick could turn dark and moody at the drop of a hat. Once at a Washington cocktail party he was slapping everybody on the back. He was in high spirits. On my way out I saw him on the curb waiting for a car, mumbling to himself. He seemed sad and detached." Ford also was fascinated at the way Nixon played piano at social functions. "There was a zest to his sing-alongs," Ford recalled. "He pounded down on the keys full-force, as if playing harder would make it sound better."[8]

Because Ford and Nixon were seeing each other socially, there was no need for an epistolary relationship. Yet one developed. After Nixon became vice president in 1953 he would occasionally drop Ford a note promoting their "friendship" and his "continued loyal support" for any legislation Ford supported. A mutual personal loyalty had been forged. But it wasn't until Nixon lost his 1962 race for governor of California that he fully appreciated what a stand-up guy Jerry really was. Most Republican politicians at the time pronounced Nixon finished, a washed-up pariah who couldn't get elected dogcatcher. Everybody enjoyed kicking Nixon while he was down — but not Gerald Ford. "I kept in touch with Dick as a friend," Ford recalled. "I knew how lonely he could get. And whenever somebody badmouthed him within my earshot I spoke up. That's what friends do for friends. When Alger Hiss went on TV and started smearing Dick I guess I spoke out."[9]

Nixon never forgot Ford's decency. "We go back a long time," Nixon wrote Ford in 1993. "As you pointed out, we are among the last of the original C & M [Chowder and Marching Club]. One action of yours for which I will always be grateful was your going on a TV program when ABC had the bad manners to put Alger Hiss on to nail my coffin shut after my defeat for governor of California. I have often said that when you win, you hear from everyone — when you lose, you hear from your friends. You have always measured up in that respect and I shall always be grateful."[10]

While his boldest peers like Kennedy and Nixon eyed the presidency during the 1950s, Ford kept his sights trained on the Speaker's chair. His pursuit inspired him to learn everything there was to know about the House of Representatives, where knowledge really *is* power, if one knows how to use it. Ford set out to find the swiftest, most surefooted route to his goal. He and John Malinowksi combed through the House archives to see who had succeeded to the top in the past. The key seemed to become a star among one's party loyalists while making a reasonable splash on a high-profile committee. He noted that three past Speakers — and President James A. Garfield — had served as chairman of the House Appropriations Committee,[11] which made sense to him, because the people who controlled the money in any endeavor tended to run the show. Ford also realized that finance generally bored the flashier types he feared most as political rivals. He thus made it his mission to get a seat on the House Appropriations Committee, and went out of his way to befriend its chairman, Democrat Clarence Cannon of Missouri, and its ranking Republican, John Taber of New York.

The problem with Ford's ambition — and the reason few freshmen in Congress would have wasted their time angling for a spot on the Appropriations Committee — was that openings were rare. To get on Appropriations, one had to break a vicious cycle; the committee members tended to keep their seats largely because their constituents didn't want them to lose their place on the powerful committee. But fortune smiled on Ford's aspirations. "As has happened so often in my life," he noted in his memoir, *A Time to Heal,* "I received a break."[12] Just as likely as also happened so often in his life, he no doubt saw it coming.

In the autumn of 1950, one of the Appropriations Committee's Republicans — a man from Michigan, coincidentally — resigned to run for a U.S. Senate seat. John Taber saw to it that Ford took his place. Given that he had not yet completed his first term, the appointment gave the young man a conspicuous boost in Congress. What's more, he instantly proved capable at work. Regarding the job as his mandate to safeguard the nation's expenditures, he followed in his adoptive father's footsteps and became adept at drawing a tight noose around every dollar he could. Unsentimentally — and, in the opinion of some of his colleagues, unwisely — Ford even voted against programs aimed to benefit the navy, Michigan, or Grand Rapids if he considered the outlay unnecessary.

The Appropriations Committee also proved an ideal vantage point for learning the workings of the House. By the time Ford finished his first full term on the committee — and his second in office — he understood more than most of his colleagues about the flow of money and power within Congress. As a near-instant insider in Washington and a rising GOP star, Ford was asked by a group of Michigan Republicans to make a bid for the Senate in 1952, against a Democrat who had been appointed to the seat after Arthur Vandenberg's death the year before. Ford seemed the perfect choice to succeed Vandenberg, both as a Grand Rapids native and as an ardent internationalist. But the congressman wasn't persuaded. The Senate had greater prestige, but the House had more real power over day-to-day legislating, especially in monetary matters. In any case, Ford felt he already had a jump on his career in the House. He saw no reason to start over in the higher chamber.

After two decades of Democratic control over the White House, Dwight D. Eisenhower won the presidency back for the Republicans in 1952. Ike's popularity across the country even spread to Congress, where the GOP squeaked into the majority by one seat in the Senate and four in the House. House Minority Leader Joseph W. Martin of Massachusetts became Speaker. A former newspaper publisher, Martin was a reasonable and congenial presence in the halls and anterooms of Congress. For the previous twenty years the Republican Party had defined itself almost entirely by contrast with the looming shadow of Franklin Delano Roosevelt, including during the administration of his successor, Harry S. Truman. Apart from the GOP's opposition to FDR — and that was hardly across the board on the issues — it was difficult to say just where the Republicans stood as the 1950s progressed. President Eisenhower didn't make it any clearer, deftly avoiding much controversy over policy. It may have been easy to like Ike, but it was tough to predict just what he would do on any particular issue.

Even at the time, both parties seemed to recognize the Eisenhower years as a frozen moment for politics as usual to take a breather after the rancorous New Deal and World War II era. Apart from the highly unusual sidelight of the Red Scare and Senator Joseph McCarthy's bullying, the 1950s passed rather placidly in Congress, but, as the decade neared its end, the American legislature roiled with the undercurrents of contention that would swell and burst through the 1960s. In the Senate, Barry Goldwater conservatives prepared to face off against Hubert Humphrey liberals.

In the House, battle lines were drawn even within the parties. In the GOP, the demarcation was generational: younger Republicans simply did not want to entrust the future to their elders in the leadership. They hadn't even held on to Ike's coattails, after all; the Democrats had retaken the House and Senate in 1954. By the end of the decade, the junior members of the House GOP believed they could do better, and organized what amounted to a coup against their leaders. Minority Leader Joe Martin, then seventy-four, was the first to be toppled, after the insurgents closed together on January 6, 1959, to challenge his twenty-year hold on the party's top spot in the lower chamber. Blunt-spoken Indiana representative Charles Halleck, fifty-seven, led the revolt. Although the genial Martin still had friends in the House, not enough voted for him this time. "A lot of us," one younger representative told the *New York Times,* "have come very reluctantly to the conclusion that we can't allow personal friendship to stand in the way of the more vigorous guidance we need."[13]

Desperate to hang on to the top office, Martin called in Ford and two of Halleck's other allies for a last-minute meeting to appeal for their support. One of them decided to stand by Martin. Gerald Ford and the other man did not. They and their like-minded peers encouraged Halleck to go forward with the coup, in hope that the House Republicans' days in the minority would end with Martin's tenure at the top.

Ford had earned a reputation as a party loyalist via his predictable obedience to the leadership, yet as old Joe Martin got the gate, Ford looked to be one of the most dangerous members of the tough-minded new cadre of younger House Republicans. Each was loyal only to his own vision of the GOP in the legislature; beyond the need for cooperation in the fight at hand, the upstarts weren't even loyal to one another. Gerald Ford's lifelong image as the most ardent of his party's faithful would stem largely from the fact that his view of the Republican Party in the House eventually prevailed. He didn't go out of his way to double-cross his colleagues, but neither would he hesitate to do just that to any who stood in his path.

As the 1960 presidential election approached, most pollsters conceded the Republican nomination to Richard Nixon, Eisenhower's vice president. Nixon nevertheless received only tepid support from the White House early on but ran as an "Eisenhower Republican" anyway — whatever that meant. What voters liked about Ike was not his adherence to ideology, liberal or conservative, but his trustworthiness in their eyes. Nixon lacked that innate appeal, and knew he would have a hard time making his "Eisenhower Republican" case. He needed another tactic for the general election.

Nixon's only competition for the GOP nomination came from New York governor Nelson A. Rockefeller, the heir to one of America's most storied fortunes, who had made himself the standard-bearer for the liberal wing of the Republican Party. When Nixon cut a deal with Rockefeller, exchanging input to the platform for the governor's support at the convention, the GOP's conservatives pitched fits.[14] The move raised suspicions of liberal sympathies in the presumptive nominee.

To balance his potential ticket, or at least give that impression, Nixon arranged for Gerald Ford's name to be circulated as a possible vice presidential nominee. Ford's record in the House certainly cast him as a reliably firm conservative, having voted against costly programs for farms, education, housing, and even the military on a few occasions. Hailing from Michigan, the center of the nation's automotive industry, however, he had enthusiastically backed the costly 1956 Federal Aid Highway Act, which created the interstate highway system, and as an avowed internationalist rarely voted against a foreign aid bill. On the domestic side, his record showed he generally favored progressive civil rights legislation, but he held a dim view of organized labor and its positions. In this mixture of stands — some conservative, some liberal — the ideologically dodgy nice-guy Gerald Ford was the epitome of an "Eisenhower Republican."

"Interest in Jerry Ford is spreading with tremendous rapidity around the country," exclaimed a Republican National Committeeman from Michigan to a reporter that spring.[15] In July, Ford arrived at the GOP convention in Chicago as Michigan's favorite son for the vice presidential nod, deplaning at Midway Airport to more than a hundred chanting, sign-waving supporters. In his final analysis, however, Nixon calculated that Ford could be of more use on his own solid turf in the House. Besides, the nominee figured, he could afford to take his party's conservatives for granted; he couldn't imagine too many of them bolting to his Democratic opponent, John F. Kennedy. So Nixon passed over his friend Jerry Ford, instead asking him to make the seconding speech for the vice presidential nomination of Boston Brahmin Henry Cabot Lodge, who brought diplomatic experience and Cold Warrior credentials to the ticket.

After the convention, Ford accepted another role in the Nixon campaign. He and two fellow House Republicans were dispatched to follow Kennedy around on the campaign trail, feeding reporters the GOP response to the Democrat's every remark. Dubbed their party's "Truth Squad," the trio's task was spin-doctoring. Ford took to his role with gusto, staunchly defending his side's platform against the dynamic Massachusetts senator. Although disappointed by Kennedy's victory that November, Ford had to admit that he still liked and admired his old hallmate in Congress, and would work closely with the new president on foreign affairs. "To know Jack Kennedy, as I did, was to understand the true meaning of the word [courage]," Ford would recall years later. "Physical pain was an inseparable part of his life, but he never surrendered to it — any more than he yielded to freedom's enemies during the most dangerous moments of the nuclear age. President Kennedy understood that courage is not something to be gauged in a poll or located in a focus group. No advisor can spin it. No historian can backdate it. For, in the age-old contest between popularity and principle, only those willing to lose for their convictions are deserving of posterity's approval."[16]

Of course, Ford's interest in presidential elections had more to do with their effect on the House of Representatives, and particularly on Republican fortunes there. Through the years he tracked the numbers of seats gained, held, and lost like a major-league baseball manager monitoring his ace's pitch count. After steadily increasing Republican losses in both houses after 1954 — capped in the 1958 midterm elections by plunges of fifteen seats in the Senate and forty-eight in the House — Ford couldn't help but be pleased that the Republicans managed to pick up two Senate seats and twenty House seats in 1960. As with Eisenhower, it appeared that Kennedy's squeaker of a victory reflected only his own popularity, and not the ascendance of his entire party. Ford could hardly wait for the midterm elections of 1962, when tradition would dictate healthy gains for the opposition party — his. But that, too, would turn out to be a disappointment, thanks to the electorate's rallying around the president during the Cuban Missile Crisis less than three weeks before the 1962 elections. The GOP dropped a pair of seats in the Senate and gained only one in the House. In response, a group of younger House Republicans concluded that, where old Joe Martin had been friendly but ineffective, the current House GOP leadership came across as antagonistic but equally ineffective.

Gerald Ford eagerly joined the upstart group, as did a brash, thirty-year-old freshman representative from Illinois named Donald Rumsfeld. Soon after the new Congress convened in January 1963, his fellow "Young Turks" urged Ford to challenge sixty-seven-year-old Charles Hoeven of Iowa for his post as chairman of the House Republican Conference. Ranking third in the GOP leadership behind Minority Leader Charles Halleck and Minority Whip Leslie Arends of Illinois, the conference chairman supposedly consulted on policy matters and helped prepare new legislation. In practice, however, the post had become little more than an honorific, with nothing much expected from its occupant. The entire House seemed taken by surprise when the forty-nine-year-old Jerry Ford announced his run for the slot. Once again, he was mounting a political power play out of ambition rather than ideology. And once again, in choosing to enter the fray, Ford proved loyal to his image of a strong Republican Party rather than to any individuals who happened to hold sway over it at the time.

"I was picked as the lamb for the slaughter," Hoeven remarked when he lost his leadership post to Ford, adding, "This should serve as notice to Mr. Arends and Mr. Halleck that something is brewing."[17] In truth, Arends was safe for the moment; it was Halleck about whom the Young Turks had misgivings. Calling himself a "gut-fighter,"[18] the tough-talking Halleck was given to high-pressure tactics, which clashed with Ford's conciliatory style, especially within the party. Halleck offended Ford more, however, with his open-armed approach to the Democratic House members from the South, conservative "Dixiecrats" who often voted with the Republicans, particularly on domestic social policy. Ford, by contrast, felt the time was ripe to regain the majority by bringing in Southern Republicans, even if backing their candidacies meant alienating a few Dixiecrats. Ultimately, he believed the result of such a shift would be a new version of the Democrats' "Solid South": still solid, but Republican in everything, including name.

On November 22, 1963, all such partisan concerns disappeared in the shadows of the assassination of John F. Kennedy. Two days after the president was shot in Dallas, the prime suspect, Lee Harvey Oswald, was himself killed by Jack Ruby, a mob-linked nightclub owner. Left with no prospect of a trial to look into the murky circumstances of Kennedy's death, the new president, Lyndon B. Johnson, announced the formation of a commission assigned "to satisfy itself that the truth is known as far as it can be discovered, and to report its findings and conclusions to him, to the American people and to the world."[19] Headed by Chief Justice Earl Warren, a Republican, the commission was made up of Democratic congressman Hale Boggs of Louisiana; Republican senator John Sherman Cooper of Kentucky; former CIA director Allen Dulles; former World Bank president John T. McCloy; Democratic senator Richard B. Russell of Georgia; and Congressman Gerald Ford. "I wanted to find who killed Jack," Ford later recalled. "I wanted the murderer put away for eternity."[20]

Ford appreciated the honor of being named to the Warren Commission, but admitted that he didn't really have time to concentrate on the investigation. "The Appropriations Committee was a full-time job," he explained in his memoirs. "The Republican Conference chairmanship demanded another hour or two every day and I didn't see how I could handle new responsibilities without obtaining additional help." He therefore deputized two aides to analyze the investigation materials as they came available, as well as to prepare questions for him to ask at the commission's hearings.[21]

Ford concurred with the Warren Commission's overall conclusion that Oswald had acted alone in the assassination of President Kennedy. As the final report on the investigation was being prepared, however, he contended that Oswald's sole culpability could not be proved by the available evidence. Thanks to Ford, the Warren Report backed away from categorically stating that there had been no conspiracy to kill JFK. Instead, the conclusion read: "The Commission has found no evidence that either Lee Harvey Oswald or Jack Ruby was part of any conspiracy, domestic or foreign, to assassinate President Kennedy."[22]

Hoping to have the last word on the matter, in 1965 Ford and John R. Stiles, one of his assistants on the ten-month investigation, coauthored a book summarizing the

Warren Commission's findings, *Portrait of the Assassin.*[23] Nevertheless, through the coming years Ford would face more questions about the Kennedy assassination investigation than any other topic. In truth, he had left the door open to all manner of conspiracy theories by inserting the clarification that the Warren Commission had "found no evidence" of a plot, thereby allowing the possibility that such evidence might exist. Indeed, when asked in 1975 on CBS's *Face the Nation* whether new disclosures warranted revisiting the investigation, Ford remarked that "if there is some additional . . . constructive information available, I think it ought to be reopened in that very limited area."[24]

In 2003, at age ninety, Ford was the only surviving member of the Warren Commission. He still bristled whenever somebody — like Hollywood director Oliver Stone — floated JFK conspiracy theories for mass consumption. "I'd like to tell you I never saw Stone's ridiculous film," Ford said. "But I was flying from New York to Los Angeles on American Airlines, and what did they show? I had no choice. The film is filled with inaccuracies and omissions. It bothered me so much because it was so wrong. But what can I do about it? At some point, I was so upset with Oliver Stone I was tempted to challenge him to a debate. I had people on my staff who said, 'All you'll do is highlight his movie and he'll get the benefit, etc.' So I backed off."[25]

In the 1964 election, Lyndon Johnson and the Democrats were able to ride on the coattails of JFK's tragic death. The national Republican Party, by contrast, hit its nadir. At the GOP convention at San Francisco's Cow Palace that July, the party's right wing seized enough control to boo Nelson Rockefeller off the podium before a word of his speech could be heard. It proved a turning point. With archconservative senator Barry Goldwater of Arizona installed at the top of the ticket, the Republicans suffered their worst electoral defeat since the 1930s. Johnson trounced Goldwater, 486 electoral votes to 52 and with 61 percent of the popular vote, on a surge of electorate support for the Democrat's proposed humanitarian Great Society programs. Jerry Ford's scorecard clearly indicated the ripple effect from what he termed Goldwater's "negative landslide."[26] The House Republicans had lost thirty-six seats. Not only were they even deeper in the minority, they were left in the dust, with 140 representatives to the Democrats' 295. Ford was frustrated; at this rate he would never get to be Speaker. Somebody had to do something to save the party, so he swung into action with his own remedy for the GOP's ills in Congress. In a January 1965 article he wrote for *Fortune* magazine, Ford laid out a new Republican strategy calling for the congressional minority to assume a more activist role, matching the Democrats' legislative efforts with constructive moderate and even liberal proposals of its own. The goal, he wrote, was to chart a course for the future, "between the shoals of simple obstructionism and inert me-tooism." What he advocated was a strong, steadfast, optimistic approach straight out of the winning playbook of Gerald R. Ford.

"We must stake out our positions independently of any preplanning with the southern Democratic leadership," he exhorted, "so as to correct the frequently distorted image of a Republican-southern Democratic coalition." To his colleagues in the House, every line of his attack was aimed straight at Charles Halleck, the right-leaning, Dixiecrat-courting minority leader. "I believe the basic Republican position we must regain is the high middle road of moderation," Ford continued. "We welcome into the party Republicans of every reasonable viewpoint. But we must firmly resist the takeover of our party by any elements that are not interested in building a party, but only in advancing their own narrow views."[27]

Ford's manifesto was more than sour grapes. He was genuinely determined to return his party to the American political mainstream. The Goldwater conservatives, who seemed more interested in airing their opinions than winning elections, had succeeded only in giving the electorate the impression that the Republican Party had swung somewhere to the right of Genghis Khan. What rankled Ford was how wide a swath this allowed the Democrats to claim in the well-reasoned ideological middle. Ford's strategy proposed to recapture the middle for his own party by pushing the opposition's image off to the left.

Just before the *Fortune* article appeared, Ford stunned Halleck with the announcement of his challenge for the minority leader's post. Few observers thought that Ford had a prayer of toppling Halleck. After all, when Representative John V. Lindsay, the erudite, liberal New York City Republican, made a few disgruntled noises of his own about his party's leadership in the aftermath of its 1964 drubbing, he was warned by his elders to stop rocking the boat. "It is impossible to rock a boat resting at the bottom of the ocean," Lindsay replied dryly.[28]

As it turned out, Ford didn't even have to rock any boats. Thanks to his bold new agenda for the party, he scored a surprise 73–67 win in the closed-door House Republican caucus vote on January 5, 1965. Front pages across the country highlighted the news, while Republican National Chairman Dean Burch quipped that it was time for the GOP to "put away the switchblades and take out the Band-Aids."[29]

Having climbed his way to the top of his party, Ford told anyone who asked, "My aim and my ambition are to be Speaker of the House of Representatives,"[30] which could only occur if the Republicans recaptured a majority of seats. Down by 155 seats, his party had a long way to go, but the GOP made progress in the 1966 congressional elections, gaining 47 House seats. Ford noted with satisfaction that the Grand Old Party "convinced the American people that we were the moderates and the president was on the left side of the spectrum." Ford's attention to the South was also paying off. "We can't win 50 percent of the House seats from only 75 percent of the country," he had railed during the midterm campaign. In January 1967 he welcomed twenty-eight new Southern Republicans to Washington.

On the day's most important issue, however, Ford and his fellows missed the chance to corner the Democrats on the Far Left. When it came to Vietnam, neither major party managed to find the sensible center. A Cold War inertia had engulfed Washington, and Ford was part of the myopia. Yet he was more cautious and reflective about the possible dire consequences of America's intervention into Southeast Asia than most of his GOP colleagues.

Ford recognized early on that the Vietnam War was taking a terrible toll on the United States, and not just in lost American lives. He often cited the latest casualty figures in his speeches, though he was certainly no antiwar dove. In fact, he advocated escalating the war effort, including an expanded aerial bombing campaign against North Vietnam. Instead of drawing distinctions between his party's position and that of the Johnson administration, Ford seemingly underlined for the electorate that all the Republicans had to offer on Vietnam was more of the same. In a rare display of political tin ear, Ford passed on the GOP's best chance to co-opt the war issue. A Senate Republican Policy Committee study released in 1967 suggested new ways to look at the political consequences of the Vietnam conflict and the possible strategies to end it. As the Senate committee report pointed out, "Republicans for two decades have believed the United States must not become involved in a land war on the Asian continent; we are so involved today."[31]

The study then tried to define the real scope of the war while questioning the Republican role in prosecuting it — opening the possibility of redefining the GOP as the party for peace in Vietnam via international diplomacy. Ford unfortunately rejected the study's ideas out of hand, maintaining that House Republicans overwhelmingly supported President Johnson on the war. They may well have, but their acquiescence to LBJ's escalations was not in the country's best interests and it certainly didn't help the Republican cause.

William Proxmire, a Democratic senator from Wisconsin, had played football on the freshman team Gerald Ford coached at Yale in the 1930s. "In many ways, [Ford] is the same kind of man now that he was then,"

Proxmire reflected, "solid and square. He is not a man of imagination."

3
FOOT SOLDIER FOR NIXON

Throughout the 1950s, Congressman Gerald Ford made national news by turning a Quonset Hut trailer into a mobile office to more efficiently service the outer reaches of his home district. In a memo directed at incoming House Republicans in 1963, he acknowledged that while tending to public relations might seem time consuming, it remained politically crucial:

> I think it's important for you to determine at the outset whether cases are a chore or an opportunity. In our office, we adopt this attitude — and sometimes I confess that it is a little difficult — but you will receive numerous communications from constituents, and at first reading you will feel that the inquiry is a bit senseless. And you wonder why he or she will have bothered you with this inquiry. In our office we always look at the inquiry from the point of

view of the person who wrote it, not from our point of view, sitting in Washington.[1]

In fact, Ford had stopped waiting for his constituents to write to him. Instead he began seeking them out. He trolled for their concerns in his mobile office, which enabled him to visit dozens of communities on a very tight schedule. With a similar openness to innovation, soon after self-developing film came on the market in 1948, Ford bought a Polaroid Land camera to keep in his Washington office so that visitors could get their pictures taken with their congressman, or seated at his desk if he was out. To Ford, a single Polaroid souvenir meant a loyal supporter for life. As House minority leader in the 1960s, Ford reached new heights in seeking voters, averaging three separate airline trips a week to speak on behalf of Republican causes and candidates — in thirty-two states in his first six months.[2] A typical such jaunt saw him completing his work on Capitol Hill around 3 p.m., dashing to Washington National Airport to get a flight to somewhere to make a speech, then racing to catch the last flight home. It would often be after midnight by the time he returned to the modest split-level home he and Betty had built in Alexandria, Virginia, in 1955. Even three decades off the gridiron, Gerald Ford still had the stamina to play the whole game, on both offense and defense.

Although Ford still had the fumbling syntax of a jock, too, his stump speeches were offset by his innate talent for public relations. He also had a knack for making people get along. As Republican conference chairman and later as House minority leader, Ford strove for cohesion and comity within his flock. Rather than strong-arm his cadre into sticking to the party line, Ford accepted differences of opinion within the fold. It made more sense to him to accommodate his members' views than splintering apart into factions. So he played the good coach, giving his squad wide latitude to speak their minds. In exchange, he wanted no bickering. Ford's open forum proved smart strategy. Whenever he needed broad cooperation on major votes, he could call on the goodwill his nice-guy approach had accrued to bring his colleagues in line.

It helped that Ford genuinely seemed less concerned about his own image than he did about the public's perception of the Republican Party. He continually reminded his team how negative publicity tended to feed on itself, and how hard it was to stop. Using the House rules and his own influence, he took pains to steer individual representatives away from fulminating on divisive issues.[3] Again, the minority leader's machinations focused on his main goal: keeping intraparty schisms from forming. In this effort he had the great advantage of never having to worry about his own reelection. Wes Vivian, a Michigan Democrat who served in the House from 1965 to 1967, told the journalist Richard Reeves, "There's an old saying that if you get more than 55 percent of the vote back home, you haven't used your potential — you could have offended more of your voters. Ford used his freedom in a different way because he wanted to be in the leadership. That's a very different thing from voting for things that might cause trouble but won't cost your seat — getting ahead internally depends on not offending anyone, avoiding entanglements, particularly ideological entanglements. You go to the gym, to the parties, you don't make enemies — it's a legitimate role inside the institution."[4]

Unlike bullying congressional leaders like Lyndon Johnson, Ford did not coerce, and he did not seek ways to punish members who voted against the party on particular bills.[5] Nevertheless, during his eight years as minority leader, fewer than a dozen House Republicans on average strayed from the GOP line on major votes.[6] His style may have been plodding but it worked. In truth, he was successful because he was so unspectacular. There was nothing threatening about Gerald Ford, which encouraged others to let their guard down around him. Many pols underestimated just how effective a tactic this could be in the U.S. Congress.

"He's an open tactician," Illinois Republican Edward J. Derwinski remarked. "He doesn't look for clever ways to sneak behind you. He does the obvious, which is usually common sense. He doesn't try to be gimmicky."[7]

Owing in part to Ford's efforts in the House, by 1968 the Republican Party seemed to be coming together on the national level. After the GOP's humiliating defeat in 1964, the vicious ideological rifts had healed to the point that the party's old standard-bearer, Richard M. Nixon, appeared likelier to top the ticket than a more controversial choice such as California's Ronald Reagan, New York's Nelson Rockefeller, or Michigan's George Romney.

In 1968 it was the Democrats' turn to fall apart. President Johnson's decision not to run for reelection opened the way for a bruising primary campaign, which was further marred by the tragic assassination of Senator Robert F. Kennedy. The party's doom seemed sealed when the whole world watched as violent riots nearly tore apart that summer's Democratic National Convention in Chicago. The Republicans' gathering in Miami was a model of decorum by comparison. After only a rustle of dissent on behalf of Reagan and Rockefeller, the party faithful fell in behind Nixon's candidacy on the first ballot. The nominee then assembled a number of GOP leaders, including Jerry Ford, in the candidate's Miami hotel suite to discuss the bottom of the ticket. Naturally, the House minority leader's name came up for the vice presidential slot. Ford remembered thinking about his now well-worn congressional scorecard. "At that moment," he wrote in his memoir, "we had 187 Republicans in the House — and we had won forty-seven of those seats two years earlier. The Democrats were terribly divided by the Vietnam War and another big Republican win seemed a strong possibility. If we captured just thirty-one more seats, I'd be Speaker of the House. I thanked Nixon for his compliment but said I wasn't interested."[8]

Privately, Ford often expressed his preference for the Speaker's post over the vice presidency. It was just as well, since Nixon didn't intend to offer him the job. Many names were bandied about as possible running mates, including Reagan, Rockefeller, and Romney, as well as Oregon's popular senator Mark Hatfield and two young politicians from Texas, Senator John G. Tower and Representative George H. W. Bush. Ford's own preference was John V. Lindsay, New York's telegenic mayor. Nixon, however, had already picked his man several weeks earlier: little-known Maryland governor Spiro T. Agnew.

A Baltimore lawyer and political operator who had been elected to his state's top job in 1966, Agnew was considered a moderate Republican. "In talking with Agnew," Nixon wrote in his presidential memoir, "I had been impressed by him as a man who seemed to have a great deal of inner strength. Though he had no foreign policy experience, his instincts seemed to parallel mine. . . . He expressed deep concern about the plight of the nation's urban areas. He appeared to have presence, poise, and dignity, which would contribute greatly to his effectiveness both as a candidate and, if we should win, as Vice President."[9]

Jerry and Betty Ford were sitting by the pool at their Miami hotel when they heard the stunning news that Nixon was putting Agnew on the ticket. In his memoir, Ford recalled thinking that Agnew "seemed like a nice enough person, but he lacked national experience or recognition. And now, after just two years as governor, he was going to run for Vice President. I shook my head in disbelief."[10] Agnew himself apparently agreed. After a brief floor battle over the choice was quashed in the interest of party unity, the vice presidential nominee proclaimed in his acceptance speech, "I stand here with a deep sense of improbability of this moment."[11]

As the 1968 GOP convention ended, national presidential preference polls indicated a wide lead for the Republican candidates over the Democratic ticket of Vice President Hubert H. Humphrey of Minnesota and Senator Edmund S. Muskie of Maine. The American Independent Party campaign of segregationist Alabama governor George C. Wallace and retired air force general Curtis LeMay, however, sapped support from the Republican right wing, leaving Nixon and Agnew struggling while the Democrats picked up steam through the autumn with promises of peace in Vietnam.

Although Nixon hung on for a slim win in November — beating Humphrey by less than one percentage point of the popular vote — his coattails pulled in only five House and six Senate seats for the Republicans. Gerald Ford, to his great disappointment, was stuck as minority leader for at least another two years. He blamed Nixon and Agnew's clumsy campaign for the paltry Republican gains in Congress. Still, Ford felt heartened that at least he would finally have a Republican White House to work with as minority leader — although that, too, would prove a terrible disappointment.

One of the most perplexing failings of the Nixon administration was its willful refusal to nurture a good working relationship with Congress, even with individual congressmen from its own party. After all, Nixon himself had served in both houses of the legislature, and thus should have been an old hand at getting things done there. Perhaps his eight years in the executive branch as vice president had given him a sense of lèse-majesté toward Capitol Hill; maybe he had gotten so used to the swift workings of his New York law practice since somewhere along the line he had lost all patience with the unwieldy Congress.

For every president, dealing with the other

end of Pennsylvania Avenue is like walking a tightrope in a shifting wind. No matter how much advance planning has been done, success still lies in sensitivity, in having the inclination as well as the skill to make adjustments at every step. By the time Nixon reached the White House, he had soured on Congress's endless wrangling to the point that he opted to ignore it in favor of the instantly effective executive-order process. Even as Ford was happily anticipating a new era of cooperation with the White House, Nixon was brooding about being "the first president in 120 years to begin his term with both houses of Congress controlled by the opposition party."[12]

With the Democrats controlling Congress, Nixon decided to consolidate executive power, largely ignoring the legislative branch on foreign affairs. The "Imperial Presidency," as Nixon's would come to be called, concentrated its power in a tiny cabal of handpicked White House aides, most of them new to Washington. Among the most influential was John D. Ehrlichman, a former land-use lawyer from Seattle whose only political loyalty was to Richard Nixon. Serving him first as counsel and later as White House Domestic Council director, Ehrlichman was in charge of the president's legislative program, working with what he called "that Congressional herd of mediocrities."[13] Ehrlichman found the House minority leader emblematic of these "mediocrities," and therefore no threat to the White House. "At my first meeting with our Republican leader in the House of Representatives, Gerald Ford, I was not impressed," Ehrlichman later wrote. "It was clear in our first conversation in 1969 that Ford wasn't thrilled to be harnessed to the Nixon Administration. Furthermore, he seemed slow to grasp the substantive information we were trying to give him. I came away from his office with the impression that Jerry Ford might have become a pretty good Grand Rapids insurance agent; he played a good game of golf, but he wasn't excessively bright."[14]

In truth, Ford was smart enough to figure out a way to keep the White House from bullying its programs through. He may not have had much imagination but he did know how to block and hold the line. His innate caution worked to his advantage in dealing with slickly aggressive types like Ehrlichman. And he wasn't about to knuckle under to any administration's arrogant disdain of the United States Congress, no matter what party they came from. Instead, he would just stall, and wait for them to learn how things were done. "As our proposals began to move to Congress," Ehrlichman noted, "I discovered that Ford, when he disagreed with Nixon's policies or programs, just didn't work on our bills." The standoff only grew tenser. In the Ninety-first Congress, the legislative branch proved relatively cooperative, voting with the White House's preferences 80 percent of the time. By the end of 1970, however, that percentage began dropping precipitously.[15] And the friction grew exponentially between Nixon and his supposed Republican friends in the House and Senate leadership.

Robert T. Hartmann, who worked on Gerald Ford's congressional staff, felt as perplexed as his boss by the attitude and atmosphere Nixon had brought to the capital. "Deep down in his heart," Hartmann averred, "Nixon had a classic case of contempt for Congress. He was a solo player; he didn't understand the power of Congress — the kind of bonding of the patriarchs. We soon found out that what Nixon wanted from the House minority leader was to do little errands for him, most of them slightly dirty; if he was attacked by Teddy Kennedy, we were supposed to get up and denounce Teddy on the House floor."[16]

If Ford felt his loyalties torn between the legislature he loved and the Republican president he seemed to be expected to serve, he had no such compunctions about taking on the judiciary. In 1969, Gerald Ford inexplicably set out to remove Associate Justice William O. Douglas from the United States Supreme Court.

The seventy-one-year-old Douglas had sat on the Court since Franklin D. Roosevelt appointed him in 1939. Douglas had a long and distinguished history on the bench, but his support for civil liberties and environmental conservation rankled many conservatives. The right wing also didn't cotton to the justice's bon-vivant lifestyle. Douglas was an obstreperous, hard-drinking womanizer who lived far beyond his salary. He made up for that in part by writing books, most of them about his travels to exotic spots around the globe. But Douglas's 1969 book, *Points of Rebellion,* analyzed and for the most part defended the rising protest movement against the Vietnam War.

Gerald Ford had been incensed by the antiwar protests for years, seeing in them "the seeds of Communist atrocity."[17] In 1968, he strongly supported passage of the Campus Disorders Act, which aimed to withhold federal subsidies from any student who took part in campus protests. When *Points of Rebellion* came out in 1969, Ford was so outraged by it that he launched an investigation into its author. That November, Ford made the shocking announcement that he was drawing up plans to impeach Douglas. It was an unprecedented assault on a justice of the Supreme Court by a member of the congressional leadership.

Earlier in 1969, Justice Abe Fortas — another liberal — had been forced to resign amid charges of financial improprieties, exposing a new level of vulnerability in the Court and among its members, which no doubt helped inspire Ford's machinations against Douglas. The search for Fortas's successor jump-started the House minority leader to keep going.

To replace Fortas, President Nixon initially nominated U.S. Appeals Court judge Clement F. Haynsworth Jr., a Southern conservative. After the Senate discovered that Haynsworth's ethical record looked at least as questionable as Fortas's, it refused to confirm him. As Indiana Democratic senator Birch Bayh — who led the rapidly growing effort to reject the nomination — pointed out, Haynsworth had "sat on cases involving litigees in which he had financial interest."[18]

It was just as the Haynsworth nomination faltered that Ford suddenly announced he was considering starting impeachment proceedings against Douglas. "If the United States Senate does establish new ethical standards for Supreme Court nominees," Ford proclaimed, "then these same standards ought to be applicable to sitting members."[19] Ford was playing a poker hand, and for much higher stakes than he was used to.

The findings he hinted at came from the investigation he had ordered into Douglas's antiwar book. The most salacious tidbit involved the publication of an excerpt in an issue of the *Evergreen Review* that also featured a pornographic photo spread. Ford also revealed that Justice Douglas had been receiving an annual salary from a foundation with ties to the Las Vegas gambling industry. But even though Ford publicly declared that his information came from independent research and with no input from the Nixon administration, the Justice Department was, in fact, feeding him leads.[20]

In April 1970, after Nixon's second choice, Court of Appeals judge G. Harrold Carswell of Florida, was rejected by the Senate (it was discovered that he had made a speech calling for white supremacy during his 1948 campaign for the Georgia legislature),[21] Ford escalated his vendetta against Douglas. Calling the justice "unfit" to serve on the nation's highest bench, Ford avowed in a speech to the House, "I would vote to impeach him right now."[22] To prove he meant business, Ford set up a special House subcommittee tasked with reassessing Douglas's ethical standing.

"It's an ugly mood," a Democratic senator told the *New York Times.* "What we seem to be witnessing is McCarthyism directed not at personalities, but institutions."[23]

The tangled reasons for Ford's bold crusade against Douglas grew out of the political complexities Richard Nixon had brought to town. It is telling that when Ford felt pressured by the Nixon administration to do something to bring Congress into line, he could not force himself to "get up and denounce Teddy," as Robert Hartmann had put it. Congress remained sacrosanct as a place for conciliation in Ford's eyes. But if he couldn't bring himself to do Nixon's bidding within the legislature, his own ambition demanded he find another way to satisfy the president.

That left the Supreme Court, and Ford's bright idea was to turn the judiciary into a low-risk, high-profile arena for partisan battles too messy to fight elsewhere. In the end, Ford's ill-considered effort to impeach Justice Douglas failed miserably, as did his larger design for the Court. What's more, after such noisy public call-to-arms the Douglas debacle left a scar on Gerald Ford's benign reputation as a generally sensible politician. Perhaps that was what Nixon had in mind: to weaken the popular GOP House leader by getting him to paint himself as a puppet of the White House. In any case, Ford's uncharacteristically mean gambit against Douglas permanently attached him to the Nixon administration, for better or for worse.

Despite Ford's protests that he had been neither asked nor ordered to mount the attack on Douglas, notes that John Ehrlichman took at a White House meeting in 1969 indicate that Nixon did indeed order his aide to instruct Ford to "move to impeach" the offending liberal justice. Furthermore, Ehrlichman recalled that he did so, the very same afternoon. If Ehrlichman's account as supported by the handwritten notes is accurate, then Gerald Ford *had* participated in the Nixon White House's dirty tricks on at least one occasion. Ford, however, didn't remember Nixon ever asking him to impeach Douglas. "Ehrlichman has no credibility on anything. I was close enough to Dick to pretty much ignore Ehrlichman and those guys, who were evil influences on him," Ford recalled. "Sometimes I would go meet Dick privately, when those guys weren't around, to speak my mind. I think he liked that I circumvented them."[24] Rather than visit the White House, Ford would sometimes meet Nixon at Andrews Air Force Base, just to welcome him home and talk policy without henchmen listening in on their private conversation. "Standing in the rain at midnight Sunday to welcome me home, as you did last evening," Nixon wrote Ford on August 4, 1969, "was far beyond the call of duty on any citizen for any President."[25]

4
THE WATERGATE
BLUES

The 1970 midterm elections marked another disaster for the Republican leader who
yearned to be Speaker of the House. The
GOP dropped twelve seats. Although the
Republicans also picked up two Senate
seats, it was no thanks to the Nixon administration, which was doing nothing to
strengthen the party as a whole. Gerald
Ford found this indifference depressing.

He had good reason. Four days after the
ballots were counted, Nixon looked to the
future — or at least to his — by calling the
first meeting to plan for his reelection bid.
In Key Biscayne on November 7, 1970,
those present included Special Assistant
John Ehrlichman, Chief of Staff H. R. Haldeman, and Attorney General John Mitchell, who would run the campaign. This
influential troika of domestic advisers
comprised the inner Nixon circle that one
Washington veteran dubbed "the Assistant

Presidents." Also in attendance were White House Senior Counsel Charles W. Colson, presidential counselor Robert H. Finch, congressional liaison P. Bryce Harlow, and hard-charging Donald H. Rumsfeld, who had resigned from Congress to join Nixon's staff.[1] Even more interesting was who was not present at the meeting. As the historian Theodore H. White pointed out in *The Making of the President 1972,* "They were there to talk politics — but no official of the Republican Party was invited."[2]

And the GOP's relations with the administration would only get chillier. "All through the campaign of 1972," White went on, "this distance between the president and his Republican Party was to grow." Senator Robert Dole of Kansas, the chairman of the Republican National Committee during the 1972 presidential campaign, couldn't even get an appointment with Nixon. Dole joked that long after he made the request he finally received a call from a presidential aide asking if he still wanted to see Nixon. Dole asked when. The aide replied, "Tune in on Channel 9, he's coming up on the tube."[3]

In the absence of any outside influence, the deliberately insular White House tended to feed on its own paranoia. The imperial mentality that took hold of the executive branch during the president's first term hardened into a zealous institutional conviction that the ends actually did justify the means. Nixon's desperate desire for reelection in 1972 didn't surprise veteran pols like Gerald Ford. The ruthlessness of his tactics, however, reflected a mind-set so genuinely twisted that, when later revealed, it would shock the nation. For the time being, the very outrageousness of what was going on in the White House was simply too incredible to be suspected.

In truth, Nixon had reason to worry about his prospects in 1972. Polls taken at the beginning of the year showed him lagging behind Senator Edmund Muskie, the Democratic front-runner. The economy had stalled while the Vietnam War continued to rip the country apart. By the end of the primary season that spring, however, Muskie's campaign had come undone, and Senator George S. McGovern, an earnest liberal from the heartland with a passionate, chaotic youthful following, was the presumptive Democratic nominee. A Harris poll conducted on May 10 showed McGovern just seven percentage points behind Nixon in a head-to-head contest.[4] Even more surprising than McGovern's ascendance was his success at raising money. As the campaign swept along into the summer, the Democrat's war chest grew fatter than the Republican incumbent's.

Richard Nixon delegated the dirty work he wanted done to his cadre of trusted aides, whose general inexperience at politics didn't deter them from throwing themselves into the campaign. Their best-known, but by no means only, attempt to rig the fall election came in the wee hours of Saturday, June 17, 1972, in the form of a burglary at the Democratic National Committee's headquarters in the Watergate office building. According to the initial news reports, three plainclothes Washington police officers, summoned by an alert security guard, entered the Democratic offices with guns drawn, surprising five men wearing rubber gloves and laden with electronic surveillance equipment, cameras, thirteen consecutively numbered hundred-dollar bills, and, on one of the men, a check signed by a sometime White House official, E. Howard Hunt. The police also found that some ceiling panels had been removed from the private office of the Democratic National Chairman, Lawrence F. O'Brien. The undercover officers took the suspicious quintet into custody on charges of second-degree burglary.

Gerald Ford was in his car later that morning when he heard a radio news report about the break-in. He was spending the weekend in central Michigan, politicking in his old-fashioned way, not with phone taps and voice-activated bugs but by showing up in person to address everything from boys' clubs to Republican state conventions. As he tooled along the highway, Ford's first reaction to the news from Washington was that the break-in had to be the work of some sort of freelance renegades. After all, no political pro would dream of taking such a foolhardy risk, or so he thought.

Spying, of course, had always played a part in politics, but caution and tradition usually confined it to planting moles and intercepting documents. That sort of gentlemen's skullduggery was prohibited under federal election law but hard to trace. Burglary, criminal trespass, and wiretapping left hard evidence. Given his firm grasp of the power of publicity, good and bad, it's little wonder that Gerald Ford called himself "flabbergasted" at the news of the break-in. "It was the most stupid political action I've known in my long career in politics," he said. "I have not the slightest idea why anybody would undertake such a stupid action."[5]

Like the rest of his countrymen, the House minority leader couldn't even conceive of anyone in the White House, much less the president of the United States, having anything to do with the crimes at the Watergate building. But by June 1972, the White House had in effect become Nixon's reelection campaign. And the vicious political tyros who ran both had none of the usual qualms about getting down and dirty. Leading the way to the new lows in American politics was John Mitchell, who had resigned as attorney general at the beginning of the month to chair the Committee to Re-Elect the President (soon to be fittingly known as CREEP).

Back in Washington that Monday, Ford began to nurse concerns about the extent and reach of the criminal activity discovered at the Watergate. Others shared his queasiness at what the D.C. police had found in the burglars' hotel room: an address book containing the phone number — marked "W.House" — of E. Howard Hunt, a known associate of Charles Colson, Nixon's close aide and counsel. Two days after the break-in at Democratic headquarters, Washington was abuzz with rumors and speculation that the Nixon administration, and possibly even the president, had had something to do with it.

Ford and some other congressional leaders happened to have an appointment that afternoon with John Mitchell. Ford managed to take Mitchell aside for a moment and asked him point-blank whether the White House had had any involvement with the Watergate burglary — and whether the president had known anything about it in advance. Mitchell adamantly replied that there was no connection. That was enough for Ford. "He looked me right in the eye," Ford remembered, "and said he had nothing to do with it — had no knowledge of it. That was pretty strong language from somebody who had been attorney general."[6]

The next day, Mitchell looked the rest of the country just as straight in the eye and disavowed any CREEP involvement in the crime. His statement responded in particular to Democratic chairman Larry O'Brien's charge that the Hunt connection between the burglars and Colson marked "a developing clear line to the White House."[7] O'Brien would be proved right in the end, but at the time his comments seemed only to politicize the debate over the Watergate affair. Two days later, on June 22, Nixon himself submitted to his first news conference in three months to assert that the White House had had nothing to do with the break-in, and that electronic surveillance "has no place whatever in our electoral process or in our governmental process."[8] Nixon loyalists quickly adopted White House press secretary Ronald Ziegler's characterization of Watergate as a "third-rate burglary attempt." To the astonishment of most Democrats and other Nixon opponents, the matter languished as a campaign issue through most of the summer.

Though some investigative reporters (notably Bob Woodward and Carl Bernstein of the *Washington Post*) were tracking the story, the next steps in the Watergate investigation would have to be taken by the government itself. Several probes were already under way, including one by the FBI, another before a federal grand jury, and three more stemming from civil lawsuits. All of these inquiries were either secret or stalled, however. Then, on September 15, 1972, the grand jury in Washington returned an eight-count indictment against the five burglars, the half-cocked CREEP operative G. Gordon Liddy, who had masterminded the burglary's logistics, and the onetime White House consultant E. Howard Hunt.

Ford had said very little about the Watergate investigations over the summer. Having been assured by John Mitchell that the ugly business didn't reach into the upper echelons of the administration, Ford had no trouble hewing to the Republican line that this third-rate burglary was nothing to talk about. So when the seven men were indicted, Ford issued a statement in conjunction with Senate Minority Leader Hugh Scott to the effect that the grand jury's action had cleared "the White House and any of the responsible people" in the Committee to Re-Elect the President."[9]

Fixated as usual on the fortunes of his party's congressional candidates across the country, Ford expended little thought on the president's campaign committee, especially given that "they wanted to reelect Nixon and didn't much care about helping anyone else."[10] In contrast to the win-at-all-costs group around Nixon, Ford was not only extremely cautious but downright proud to call himself a professional pol. The Watergate scandal was simply not in Gerald Ford's ken, and he treated it as a minor affair. This was evident in Ford's role in Congress's earliest effort to shed light on the scandal, through what would be known as the Patman Committee.

Representative Wright Patman was a silver-tongued seventy-nine-year-old Texan bursting with energy. As the Democratic chairman of the House Banking and Currency Committee, he took a special interest in the money trail leading from the Watergate burglars through several banks, including one in Mexico, to high-ranking officials at the Finance Committee to Re-Elect the President (FCREEP). During the summer of 1972, Patman and his staff compiled an eighty-page report detailing the flow of some $10 million in otherwise undocumented cash into various CREEP safes and accounts. Those shady dealings alone were enough to constitute a violation of federal election law, but the report also corroborated the connections among FCREEP, the Mexican bank account, and the funding of the Watergate break-in. Patman proposed that his committee subpoena a number of high CREEP officials, including FCREEP chairman Maurice Stans and John Mitchell, who had stepped down as CREEP chairman on July 1. In his diary entry for September 15, 1972, H. R. Haldeman noted that Nixon "wants to be sure we put the screws on Congress to turn off the Patman hearings."[11]

Patman was set to open the first public hearings on Watergate in October 1972. In order to proceed, however, he needed a majority vote to do so from the members of his full committee. In terms of House procedure, it was right for him to hold such hearings — the irregularities under investigation had occurred earlier that year and the relevant witnesses were readily available for questioning. In political terms, with the presidential election just a month away, Patman's timing made his inquiry explosive. White House Counsel John W. Dean III was in charge of mitigating the effects of the various Watergate investigations. At a September 15 meeting with the president and Haldeman, Dean warned: "Patman's hearings — his Banking and Currency Committee — whether we will be successful in turning that off or not I don't know."

After discussing several options for quashing the congressional committee hearings the trio turned to the subject of the House minority leader's potential usefulness:

Dean: Jerry Ford is not really taking an active interest in this matter that is developing, so Stans is going to see Jerry Ford and try to brief him and explain to him the problems he has. The other thing we are going to do — we are looking at all the campaign reports of every member of that committee, because we are convinced that none of them complied exactly with the law either. If they want to play rough, someday we'd better say, "Gentlemen, we want to call [to] your attention that you have not complied with A, B, C, and F, and we are not going to hold that a secret if you start talking campaign violations here."

Nixon: What about Ford? Do you think so? . . . If Ford can get the minority members — they have some weak men and women on that committee, unfortunately. [Republican Representative Margaret] Heckler [of Massachusetts] is all right.

Dean: Heckler was great.

Nixon: [Republican Representative William] Widnall [of New Jersey], etcetera. Jerry should talk to Widnall. After all, if we ever win the House, Jerry will be the Speaker and he could tell him if he did not get off — he will not be Chairman, ever.

Dean: That would be very helpful, to get all of these people at least pulling together. If Jerry could get a little action on this . . .

Haldeman: Damn it, Jerry should. That is exactly the thing he was talking about — that the reason they are staying is so that they can run investigations.[12]

As September turned to October, Ford

began lobbying Republican members of the Banking and Currency Committee to vote against Patman's hearings. He told his colleagues that an open inquiry at that moment could compromise the pending trials of the seven Watergate defendants. In truth, the matters under scrutiny in the two proceedings involved entirely separate issues, so the Patman investigation would in no way have affected the trials. Nevertheless, Ford succeeded in squelching Patman's plans. All sixteen Republican members of the Banking and Currency Committee voted against holding the hearings, and four Democrats joined them. The final vote was 20 to 15 against the lively old Texan.

According to Republican representative Garry Brown, who also played an active role in the effort, Ford cooperated with the Justice Department to block the Patman Committee hearings.[13] The tape recording of the September 15 Oval Office meeting supports John Dean's charge, which Ford refuted, that the minority leader also acted in conjunction with the White House. It also seems telling that Ford evinced no interest in the matter until right after that White House meeting to plan the Watergate cover-up effort. But he had received a September 6 letter from the president slyly noting that, "You looked so good on television while presiding [at the GOP convention] that I became more convinced than ever that you would make a *great Speaker* [emphasis in original]."[14]

Ford, of course, had good reason to cooperate with the administration in stifling Wright Patman. As minority leader, it was part of his job to act as point man on party concerns in the House. With his keen grasp of political give-and-take, Jerry Ford knew that he had to choose his battles, and fight at least a few that really mattered to Nixon. So while he just didn't pursue some matters brought up to him by the White House, as Ehrlichman and others who worked with him complained, he gave the obstruction of Wright Patman his all.

Despite Republican panic at the kind of damage public hearings could do just five weeks before the presidential election, the Watergate scandal stirred little interest outside the most partisan Democratic circles. In that sense, the White House cover-up proved a triumph. On November 7, 1972, Richard Nixon crushed George McGovern, winning 520 electoral votes. If it was vindication for his checkered political past that Nixon was looking for, he certainly found it that election day. But the huge victory turned out to be largely Nixon's alone. The president had become the first Republican candidate since Reconstruction to sweep what had once been the Democrats' "solid South," at the same time making deep inroads with the opposition's traditional coalition of labor, youth, blacks, Jews, Catholics, and the poor. Yet, despite his juggernaut, the Republican Party actually lost two seats in the Senate and picked up only twelve in the House, leaving the Democrats still in control with a fifty-seat majority. For all President Nixon's flattery that he would be great at the job, Gerald Ford was still not going to be Speaker of the House.

Like many other Republicans outside the White House, Ford felt betrayed by what one reporter called Nixon's "to-hell-with-the-party" attitude. Quietly, he began to let go of his dream of the top job in Congress. In fact, he had grown so frustrated that after discussing his future with his wife, Betty, he decided he would leave Washington politics in January 1977. His plan was to spend two more years as minority leader and then a final term out of the congressional leadership.

CREEP's no-holds-barred effort in the presidential race may have resulted in a landslide victory but it came at a high cost.

Ignoring and even antagonizing his party's faithful had left Nixon in bad odor with his fellow Republicans in Congress. In consequence, when the Senate was considering holding hearings on Watergate in early 1973, eighteen Republicans voted in favor with the Democrats. For Nixon, finding GOP allies on Capitol Hill became nearly impossible. In truth, for the president it was increasingly hard to find friends anywhere. Between the even more zealous news coverage of Watergate and the revelations of the Senate Select Committee on Presidential Campaign Activities, the public slowly began to realize that much of what they had heard from the administration about Watergate had been a pack of lies. More Republicans started speaking out openly against Nixon, angered by the damage he and his henchmen had done to the party, to the integrity of the nation's highest office, and ultimately to the Constitution of the United States. The ever-cautious Jerry Ford did not go nearly that far. Instead he continued to defend the president, while encouraging Nixon's top aides to clear their names of suspicion by appearing under oath before the Senate Select Committee.[15]

Ford would later claim that his faith in the administration continued because he still believed John Mitchell's personal assurance the previous June. But a year later, the tangled web of outrages spun out of the White House had grown far beyond the burglary at Democratic National Committee headquarters. By the summer of 1973, the term "Watergate" had swollen to encompass a dizzying litany of dirty tricks, shady financial deals, and other downright felonious activities. But if any of the cascading revelations of malfeasance in the White House made Ford doubt Mitchell's original refutation, he did not let on in public. While other Republicans of all stripes avidly questioned Nixon's role in the scandal, Ford stood his ground behind the president.

His fealty would soon pay off. On August 6, 1973, in the midst of Watergate and yet entirely separate from it, the stunning news broke that Vice President Spiro Agnew was under investigation for bribery, conspiracy, and tax evasion. Although Agnew loudly proclaimed his innocence, federal prosecutors in Baltimore already had the goods on him: that as a county executive in 1966 he had taken payoffs from Baltimore County contractors, then done the same thing as Maryland's governor, and then again even as vice president. What's more, Agnew had failed to pay income tax on the kickbacks.[16]

The examination of Agnew's financial misdeeds had been under way since February, but when it became public the vice president found himself in a fight not just for his political future but for his physical freedom as well. A conviction on such charges would carry serious jail time.

Faced with this fresh crisis, the administration made a halfhearted effort to save Agnew. In September Nixon pretty much turned the Agnew matter over to Attorney General Elliot Richardson, who took the hard line of negotiating a plea bargain contingent on the vice president's resignation. Agnew tried to put up a fight at first, but even he wasn't obtuse enough to see that he was snared between an understandably nervous administration and a team of federal prosecutors armed with solid evidence. As one lawyer familiar with the details of the investigation put it, he'd "never seen a stronger extortion case."[17] Just two months after the inquiry became public, Agnew was done for. He was fined $10,000 for the income-tax evasion. Agnew's lawyers worked out a deal with the Nixon administration and the prosecutors: the vice president would resign but not go to jail.

Thus on October 10, 1973, Spiro Agnew

resigned the vice presidency, with hardly a word to his former colleagues in the White House. Given the adversarial climate in the country, Nixon understood that he could not make another mistake with the choice of his next number-two man. Not only had Americans had it with political turmoil but the Twenty-fifth Amendment — in place, fortuitously, only since 1967 — gave Congress the power to confirm the president's choice. No one unqualified to hold the top job would be allowed to slip into the understudy's role this time, and Nixon knew it. The president immediately began soliciting recommendations for Agnew's replacement. He assiduously appealed to Republican leaders at all levels for advice, inviting every GOP member of Congress, governor, national committee member, and state party chair to list up to three potential candidates in a sealed letter to the White House. Nixon wanted to find a quickly confirmable choice as soon as possible; until the new vice president was sworn in, Speaker of the House Carl Albert, an Oklahoma Democrat, stood next in line to take over the presidency.

The party leaders' suggestions reflected the perennial post-Eisenhower split in the GOP: Nelson Rockefeller from the liberal wing and conservative Ronald Reagan were virtually tied for first place. Former Texas governor and Treasury Secretary John Connally (Nixon's preference) came in third, but he was also too controversial to nominate, having switched his affiliation from the Democratic to the Republican Party only earlier that year. (In other words, no one in Congress could trust him.) In fourth place was Jerry Ford.

The House minority leader, however, received the most important vote, aside from that of Nixon himself. The man who held the position Ford really wanted — Speaker Albert — told the president straight out that Ford would breeze the easiest through the congressional confirmation process. That, plus his internationalist foreign policy views, made Ford an acceptable and practical choice to Richard Nixon. The president, congenitally paranoid in the best circumstances, had every reason to think everyone was out to get him. And as his position continued to weaken, Nixon found ever fewer colleagues he could count on to remain loyal both to him and to his office.

Ford was, in essence, a welcome anomaly. Thus it was with sincere satisfaction all around that Nixon summoned Jerry Ford to the White House on October 12, and after a short discussion asked him to become his vice presidential nominee. Ford was ready with his acceptance, seeing the nation's number-two job as a fitting place to end his career in Washington, after a quarter century in Congress. It didn't seem to bother him that he was leaving the legislature just as it was entering its finest hour as the guardian of the Constitution to become part of an administration on the verge of collapse.

5
CHANGING OF THE GUARD

"The person with the best job in the country is the vice president," humorist Will Rogers once said. "All he has to do is get up in the morning and ask, 'How is the president?' " That quip took on a darker double meaning during Gerald Ford's eight months in the office. Never before had an American vice president, whose position John Adams called "the most insignificant office that ever the invention of man contrived," been so important.[1] Ever the regular guy, Ford himself downplayed the point in his speech upon being sworn in on December 6, 1973. Yet an artful assurance informed the humility in his declaration that, "I am a Ford, not a Lincoln. . . . I am proud — very proud — to be one of the two hundred million Americans. I promise my fellow citizens only this: to uphold the Constitution, to do what is right as God gives me to see the right, and, within the limited powers and duties of the vice presidency, to do the very best that I can for America."[2]

He got the job because his former colleagues in Congress believed him. As liberal senator Alan Cranston of California said for many at Ford's confirmation vote on November 27: "Frankly, I am astonished to hear myself, a life-long Democrat, support a Republican for Vice President . . . [but Gerald Ford] has come into focus as someone who appears to offer the nation a steadiness and a dependability for which it yearns. I doubt if there has ever before been a time when integrity has so surpassed ideology in the judging of a man for so high an office."[3] Indeed, Ford got tapped, as Charles W. Colson later reminded investigative journalist Seymour Hersh, because "Nixon knew that Ford was a team player and understood how to work with a wink and a nod."[4]

Just before announcing his vice presidential choice on October 12, Nixon had listed his criteria for his new understudy as follows: "must be qualified to be president . . . must share the view of the president on critical issues of foreign policy and national defense," and must be "an individual who can work with members of both parties in Congress." When the East Room erupted in cheers after Nixon named Jerry Ford as that man, a microphone near the pair picked up the president telling his new vice president, "They like you." To which Ford matter-of-factly replied, "I have a couple of friends out there."[5]

That was the idea: the vice president's principal duty, besides standing by, is to serve as president of the Senate, and as such Ford would be Nixon's ambassador to Congress. In truth, he started in that capacity at his confirmation hearings, proposing to serve as "a ready conciliator and calm communicator between the White House and Capitol Hill, between the reelection mandate of the Republican President and the equally emphatic mandate of the Democratic 93rd Congress." Comity among the branches of government, Ford asserted, stood as "the single greatest need of our country today."[6]

As vice president, Ford had been led to expect that he would serve President Nixon on Capitol Hill, as a sort of uber-lobbyist for the administration's positions on pending legislation. In practice, however, Ford found himself only occasionally handling congressional matters. Most of his time instead went to doing what he liked best: stumping across the country for the Republican cause, which at that point was the survival of Nixon's presidency. In his eight months as vice president, Ford flew 118,000 miles to make nearly five hundred personal appearances in forty states. "No event was too small," remembered NBC News correspondent Ron Nessen, "from the dedication of a container wharf in New Orleans to a St. Patrick's Day dinner for the Hibernian Society in Charleston, South Carolina, to a lunch with seventh graders in Honolulu." Nessen, who would become Ford's White House press secretary in September 1974, added, "There was a joke during that period: If you were having a banquet and you couldn't get the local chief of police to speak, ask Vice President Ford."[7] On some days his hectic road schedule saw him attending ten different events in four or five states, all to promote Nixon's innocence and, secondarily, the GOP line on issues.[8]

He also didn't mind taking on Agnew's arch role as the administration's fire-breather against the media and the left. In January 1974, a month after taking office, the new vice president gave a chest-thumping speech for the American Farm Bureau Federation in Atlantic City, one that sounded nothing like good ol' Jerry Ford. That was because he didn't write it. Conservative White House scribe Patrick J. Buchanan did, making no adjustments to the stridency he had defined for Spiro Agnew.[9] By delivering Buchanan's screed as supplied, Ford put himself firmly and combatively on the side of Nixon's apologists. In Atlantic City he blamed the president's problems on "powerful pressure organizations" such as the AFL-CIO and Americans for Democratic Action. "If they can crush the president and his philosophy, they are convinced that they can then dominate the Congress and, through it, the nation," Ford said of these "extreme partisans" trying to bring down the chief executive with "a massive propaganda campaign."

Ford's speech made news around the country, in part because of its uncharacteristic vitriol. Even more noteworthy was the timing of the new vice president's attack. That day, Americans found themselves facing the most damning evidence yet of a White House cover-up, but Ford was ascribing the entire Watergate crisis to the ill intent of a "relatively small group of activists."

Over the previous two months, investigators had been homing in on an eighteen-and-a-half-minute gap in the Oval Office recording of a June 20, 1972, meeting between President Nixon and Chief of Staff H. R. Haldeman. The blank portion came in the middle of what might have been a telling conversation about the break-in at Democratic National Committee headquarters. On the day of Ford's pro-Nixon rant in Atlantic City, a team of audio experts released their conclusion that the gap in the tape had been created by at least five separate acts of erasure, all of which almost certainly could not have been accidental — Haldeman's successor, Alexander M. Haig Jr., attributed it to "some sinister force."[10] It now looked like the White House had destroyed evidence. As Michigan's own *Detroit News* observed, "The new evidence pulls the rug from under the President's loyal apologists."[11]

Clearly, Ford had not known about the audio experts' report when he read Buchanan's harsh speech on January 15; the findings became public a few hours after he addressed the farmers. Even so, Ford would not back away from his comments. The *Detroit News* thus continued: "While the latest horror story was being told in Judge Sirica's court, Vice President Gerald Ford, doing his best to restore confidence in the administration, was out delivering a speech in which he blamed a few extreme partisans

110

for stretching out the ordeal of Watergate for their own political purposes."[12]

After the audio experts' report, Ford would nevertheless go on protesting the president's complete innocence. Many of his most trusted associates advised Ford to tone down his insistence to that effect, warning that he was only damaging his own credibility. While not abandoning his defense of Nixon, Ford did adopt a less strident tone in his later speeches.

No other U.S. vice president had ever been put in such a politically sensitive position. As the nation's second in command, Ford couldn't say a word against Nixon without looking like he was after his boss's job. In that regard, staying loyal served his own interests, too. Even so, Ford could easily have opted to say less rather than more, cutting back on his public appearances and replying blandly to any unavoidable questions about Watergate. Instead, for some reason he refused to take the safer course. "Somebody ought to do Jerry Ford a favor and take his airplane away from him," the *Wall Street Journal*'s Norman Miller wrote on June 4.[13]

But no one did, and Ford's vice presidency turned into a better-attended replay of his service as House minority leader. "Ford was living like a super-congressman who did not even have to show up for roll call votes," wrote the reporter Richard Reeves. Not that his travels offered much glamour: "Gerald Ford's America," Reeves continued, "was a mind-blurring parade of middle-aged men in double-knit suits — the small business-men and corporate executives who are the core and soul of the Republican party — holding plastic cups of Scotch at $25-a-couple receptions in the Windsor Rooms of motels outside medium-sized cities. After one of those long nights, I asked him if he planned to see and hear non-Republican Americans, and he answered that he already had. 'I'm going to have a private meeting tomorrow with another nonpartisan group, the directors of the Hearst Corporation.' "[14]

To explain his firm stance on Watergate, Ford later claimed that he often harked back to his private talk with John Mitchell in June 1972. "Quite honestly," Ford maintained in retrospect, "that assurance from him was a factor in my strongly supporting Nixon up till the last."[15] Ford's faith in that assurance did not waver even after March 1, 1974, when Mitchell was indicted by a federal grand jury on charges of obstruction of justice and conspiracy, along with three counts going to his sheer mendacity: perjury, making false declarations, and lying to the FBI.

But at the same time that Ford was defending Nixon by insisting that no impeachable offenses had been committed, he was also suggesting the president would be wise to turn over the White House tapes and other materials to the Watergate investigators. He had told the Senate Judiciary Committee during his vice presidential confirmation hearings that he believed that impeachment proceedings should begin, "if for no other reason than to clear the air."[16] If Ford was indeed on a campaign, that was its platform: that the president was innocent beyond reproach, and to prove it he ought to be entirely forthcoming. "The preponderance of the evidence," as Ford liked to call it, "is in favor of the President and exonerates him of any impeachable offense."[17] Ford, of course, did not know that for certain. He had not heard the most damning of the tapes, and neither had anyone else — not even Nixon's personal attorneys.

In truth, the vice president did not want to hear the tapes in Nixon's possession, and scrupulously avoided every opportunity to do so.[18] If he did hear the evidence, after all, he could hardly keep waging the campaign he had taken up, which he summarized in a remark at Harvard University in March 1974: "I don't happen to believe on the basis of the evidence I am familiar with — and I think I'm familiar with most of it — that the President was involved in Watergate *per se* or involved in the cover-up, but time will tell."[19] As Nixon began to fall, Ford thus kept himself carefully positioned on the sidelines, where his view of Watergate looked not much closer than that of the American public. To many observers, the new vice president looked an outright fool for continuing to proclaim Nixon's innocence.[20]

If Ford was a fool, he was the same ploddingly loyal GOP fool he had remained throughout his entire political career, and what a career it had turned out. Calling him "the very model of a modern American politician," Richard Reeves wrote, "His success was a triumph of lowest-common-denominator politics, the survival of the man without enemies, the least objectionable alternative. The remarkable thing about Ford and others like him is that they have won leadership by carefully avoiding it. The act and art of leading inevitably offends and alienates some of the people some of the time in a democratic universe," but Ford "built his career and life on avoiding offending anyone." Of course, as Reeves noted, Ford was also the kind of politician to remark of Republican Representative John B. Anderson of Illinois, "He's the smartest guy in Congress, but he insists on voting his conscience instead of party."[21] It's little wonder that H. R. Haldeman's diary entry for May 18, 1971, had noted that Nixon "got into quite a long thing on the lack of leadership in the Congress . . . making the point that Gerry Ford really is the only leader we've got on either side in either house."[22]

Thus in the spring of 1974, to the extent that he was waging a campaign, Ford's efforts were actually aimed at a constituency of one: Richard M. Nixon. His success was marked in the following handwritten missive from the president dated June 8, 1974. "This is just a note to tell you how much I have appreciated your superb and courageous support over these past difficult months," Nixon wrote Ford. "How much easier it would be for you to pander to the press and others who desperately are trying to drive a wedge between the President and the Vice President. It's tough going now, but History will I am sure record you as one of the most capable, courageous, and honorable Vice Presidents we have ever had."[23]

On July 24, the Supreme Court ruled 8 to 0 that President Nixon had to surrender an additional sixty-four tapes and documents subpoenaed by special prosecutor Leon Jaworski "forthwith." Even Nixon's own lead attorney, James St. Clair, wasn't certain what was on the tapes — to the annoyance of Judge John J. Sirica, who claimed bafflement over a lawyer's waging such a spirited battle to protect recorded conversations he had not even heard. Thus, on July 26, Sirica actually ordered St. Clair to remedy that gap in his preparation. Even the drama over the tapes, however, paled beside the next move from the House Judiciary Committee, which on July 27 voted in favor of the first of three articles of impeachment, charging the president with conduct intended to impede the Watergate investigation. The vote came out 27 to 11, with six of the committee's seventeen Republicans joining all twenty-one of its Democrats.

There was no turning back: President Nixon was headed for impeachment, if not yet convicted of anything. Later that day, Ford pallidly observed to the press that "the fact that every one of the Democrats on the committee voted for it lends credence that it's a partisan issue, even though some Republicans voted for it." He added that Nixon should "do as he has done: indicate as clearly as he can that he is innocent."

Over that last weekend of July 1974, St. Clair finally heard the tape of the "smoking gun" conversation of June 23, 1972, just six days after the break-in, in which Nixon had told Haldeman to block the FBI's Watergate investigation. Before the tape ended he knew the case was over. Nixon could clearly be heard leading the discussion about hindering the investigation of the break-in. The president not only knew about the cover-up — itself an obstruction of justice, and thus a felony — but he had directed it. Upon reading the transcript of the conversation, even White House Chief of Staff Alexander Haig threw in the towel. "I just don't see how we can survive this one," he told the president. "The facts are that the staff won't hold and that public opinion won't either, once this tape gets out."[24]

Nixon reported in his memoirs that he made his decision to resign the nation's highest office on Tuesday, July 30. Other sources suggest he continued to weigh his options all the rest of that week. In his diary entry for July 31, Republican National Committee Chairman George H. W. Bush recorded that Haig had summoned him to the White House to discuss the likelihood that Nixon would in fact not resign. Bush also noted that "Haig was terribly complimentary of Ford and the job he was doing, indicating that he was one of the best things the President had ever done."[25] Haig met with Ford and his chief of staff Robert Hartmann that Thursday, August 1, to apprise them of the contents of the "smoking gun" tape and the pall it cast over Nixon's chances of staying on as president. Haig wasn't through, however. He also arranged to meet with Ford privately later that same day, with a more specific agenda. On the assumption that Nixon had to resign, Haig outlined a number of possible exit scenarios for the president, including several that involved his pardon. According to Haig's legal research, Nixon could pardon himself before leaving office, or his successor could pardon him at some later point. The vice president said that he would think over the possibilities.

Ford has maintained ever since that no deal for a pardon was struck at his private meeting with Haig. There was no reason to be that explicit; Haig needed only to note that the vice president did not balk at the notion. Even Ford quickly realized how critical that subtle point might seem under the circumstances. The next day, after speaking with Hartmann and other advisers, he felt compelled to call Haig to clarify that he wanted no part in formulating Nixon's course of action, especially regarding the president's resignation, and that no assumptions should be made about a pardon from his successor.

In any event, Ford knew that Nixon's days were numbered.

Nonetheless, that Saturday found Gerald Ford in Hattiesburg, Mississippi, telling reporters, "I believe the president is innocent of any impeachable offense and I haven't changed my mind."[26] As he had yet to hear the incriminating tape firsthand, Ford thus stayed within the bounds of his own ethics, where the line was drawn between what he knew for certain and what he had learned only by hearsay. But his remarks in Hattiesburg constituted an unsavory exercise in technically telling the truth while at the same time perpetuating a lie. By August 3, Ford knew perfectly well that Nixon was not innocent. Still, and perhaps more so than even he realized, he fell prey to Richard Nixon's inordinate demand for loyalty at all costs. Doing so had ruined dozens of others — but not Gerald Ford. Over his long congressional career Ford had built up what seemed an unassailable reputation. As Bush put it in his diary on August 6, "this era of tawdry, shabby, lack of morality has got to end. . . . I will take Ford's decency over Nixon's toughness because what we need at this juncture in our history is a certain sense of morality and a certain sense of decency."[27]

On Monday, August 5, Nixon released a transcript of the fatal tape. At that point Ford finally jumped ship, at least insofar as he admitted that "the public interest is no longer served by repetition of my previously expressed belief that on the basis of all the evidence known to me and the American people, the President is not guilty of an impeachable offense."[28] He was quick to add that he hadn't read the transcript of that tape yet. Ford's conviction that ignorance was his smartest course held firm. The next morning, while most of the nation pored over the transcripts published in newspapers across the country, the vice president, who could have had an advance copy for the asking, chose for the moment to keep seeing no evil.

On Thursday, Ford was summoned to the Oval Office to meet with President Nixon at 11 a.m. "The President's face was ashen, but his voice was controlled and measured," wrote Jerald F. terHorst. "The two men shook hands and Nixon motioned Ford to the chair beside him. There was an awkward moment. Then Nixon broke the silence: 'I know you'll do well,' he said. Ford nodded silently. The Presidency had passed from one man to the other."[29]

After agreeing that Secretary of State Henry Kissinger should remain in his post, the pair spent the next hour chatting nonchalantly about the quarter century they had shared in politics and as friends. Ford later revealed that he felt only sadness at his old pal's plight that morning, and no joy for himself. As he had made no effort to do so, he claimed, becoming president of the United States hardly seemed a triumph. That evening, August 8, 1974, in a televised address to the nation, Richard Nixon announced that he would resign its highest office the next morning. Gerald Ford was about to learn what Thomas Jefferson meant when he wrote, "The second office of the government is honorable and easy, the first is but a splendid misery."[30]

On Friday morning, August 9, the president's formal resignation was submitted to the secretary of state as Nixon flew off to his exile in San Clemente, California. At three minutes after noon, Chief Justice Warren E. Burger swore in Gerald R. Ford as the thirty-eighth president of the United States. With a notable lack of ceremony in the White House East Room, Ford delivered a short but pitch-perfect inaugural address, telling his scandal-weary nation, in part: "I assume the presidency under extraordinary circumstances never before experienced by Americans. . . . I am acutely aware that you have not elected me as your president by your ballots and so I ask you to confirm me as your president in your prayers. . . . I have not sought this enormous responsibility, but I will not shirk it. I believe that truth is the glue that holds government together, not only our government but civilization itself. That bond, though strained, is unbroken at home and abroad. In all my public and private acts as your president, I expect to follow my instincts of openness and candor with full confidence that honesty is the best policy in the end.

"My fellow Americans, our long national nightmare is over."[31]

6
THE PARDON MEETS WHIP INFLATION NOW

Ford's inauguration was eclipsed by Nixon's teary farewell that same day, with the media portraying Ford as a dull coda to the monstrous Nixon saga. The image of a lip-biting Nixon flashing the double-victory sign from the steps of his helicopter was immediately seared onto the national memory for posterity. Nobody heard Ford leaning <u>over</u> and whispering into his wife's ear, "We can do it!" Aside from Washington, Lincoln, and FDR — America's big three — it's difficult to recall a president who took office amid less favorable circumstances. The true public courage exhibited that day didn't emanate from Nixon fleeing Washington but from Ford, who was anxious to heal a deeply divided nation. He was being asked to assume the presidency in a White House sinking in the quicksands of Vietnam and Watergate. Ford said "yes" not because he wanted power but because it was his duty.

The new president's White House transition team wasted no time removing every visible trace of Richard Nixon from the Oval Office, scurrying about replacing his mementos with photographs of Gerald Ford in notable company and settings. The transfer of power had been elegantly executed in accordance with the U.S. Constitution. Capitalizing on the sense of pride in America this had engendered, President Ford began by revolutionizing the presidency's political style. By quickly highlighting his contrasts with Nixon, Ford redefined the public image of the office as well. "Within an hour of his swearing-in," Jerald F. terHorst reported, "Ford appeared in the White House press room, where he told waiting reporters of his hopes 'for the kind of rapport and friendship we've had in the past. And I don't ask you to treat me any better. We will have an open . . . and candid Administration. I can't change my nature after sixty-one years.' "[1]

Where Nixon had barricaded himself in the White House behind the shield of "executive privilege," Ford spent most nights during his first week as leader of the free world at his house in suburban Alexandria, Virginia. News photographers clicked away madly early his first full day as president when Ford came out on his front step in his pajamas to get the morning paper.[2]

Everything about the chief executive had changed — except, at first, the top personnel advising the president. Ford, a firm believer in the collegial approach to decision making, kept on Nixon's entire cabinet and White House staff, in the interest of continuity. Two of the holdovers immediately asserted their claims to what had been their considerable turf under Nixon. The first to stake out his territory was Secretary of State Henry Kissinger, who portentously warned Ford that any change in U.S. foreign policy — which was to say, in Kissinger's foreign policy — would betray America's Watergate-weakened state to the world, with potentially dire consequences. "Henry is a genius," Nixon had told Ford before resigning, "but you don't have to accept everything he commends. He can be invaluable, and he'll be very loyal, but you can't let him have a totally free hand."[3]

Ford didn't need Nixon to convince him that Kissinger was a genius diplomatist. Back in the early 1960s, when Ford was head of the House Defense Appropriations Subcommittee, Kissinger, then a Harvard professor, used to invite the Michigan congressman to address his class. "I was really impressed with the guy," Ford recalled. "We had some wonderful times together in Cambridge. He was smarter than me and I liked that about him. Later we'd see each other in New York or Washington, D.C. I was fond of him. Not everybody can make you think and laugh at the same time."[4]

Next to make his work known was Chief of Staff Alexander Haig, who "made it clear that he had been running the government for the last eight or ten months of the Nixon Presidency," according to terHorst, who was about to become Ford's White House press secretary.[5] The former army general left a strong impression with his snap-to manner and crisp grasp of White House operations. The new president soon took to leaning heavily on Haig's judgment, to the dismay of the long-standing advisers Ford had brought with him from his congressional staff. At the Republican National Committee, George H. W. Bush remained cautiously hopeful that Ford would build a solid White House. "My own views are that the Vice President can make it as President," Bush confided to his diary on August 6. "He is a latter-day Eisenhower . . . without the heroics but he has that decency the country is crying out for right now."[6]

Ford left no doubt about his desire to

change the executive branch with his first and most important political appointment, which he had to make as soon as possible. For the second time in a year the vice presidency was vacant, meaning that Speaker of the House Carl Albert would be in the White House should anything happen to Gerald Ford. After listening to the suggestions of many advisers, the new president went with his own gut in picking his understudy. On August 20 he nominated former New York governor Nelson A. Rockefeller, the multimillionaire GOP liberal. Rockefeller had little in common with the Midwestern conservative president whose dad had sold paint for a living. In fact, he disagreed with Ford on many policy issues. But "Rocky" had star quality and Ford's PR instincts told him that was what his new administration needed most. The bumptious, broad-grinning Rockefeller was the civic-minded icon of a genuine American dynasty, with merry eyes behind his big, square black glasses, and a deep interest in global affairs. "Even with governors like Franklin Roosevelt and Thomas Dewey," Richard Reeves reported, "New York had never had a foreign policy until Rockefeller came along."[7]

Meanwhile, the American people accorded Ford a honeymoon for simply *not being* Richard Nixon. The new president enjoyed sky-high popularity ratings. A Gallup poll commissioned by the *New York Times* in late August showed that 71 percent of those surveyed approved of his performance, with only 3 percent disapproving.[8] Ford immediately took advantage of his popularity. First, he made a genuine effort to reach out to groups that traditionally did not support Republicans. He saw himself primarily as a conciliator, and sincerely wanted to mend the old rips in the nation's fabric. He courted African-American political leaders, inviting the Congressional Black Caucus to meet with him at the White House just three days into his presidency. Ford also invited AFL-CIO president George Meany in to talk about labor issues. "I wasn't considered pro–Big Labor," Ford recalled. "But I respected the power of Big Labor."[9]

Then, at the Veterans of Foreign Wars national convention in Chicago, on August 19, Ford overturned a firm Nixon policy, proposing conditional amnesty for Vietnam War draft dodgers and deserters. "I am throwing the weight of the presidency on the side of leniency," he announced. Coming from a conservative Republican who had once been as hard on Vietnam protesters as any politician in the country, Ford's amnesty announcement was surprisingly well received, and his popularity remained high. "The VFW speech was the most striking example to date that Richard Nixon was gone," Richard Reeves observed, "showing a President compassionately aware of the divisions among Americans."[10]

But Nixon didn't stay gone for long, and his reemergence as a public issue dramatically ended Ford's honeymoon. To Ford's chagrin, at his first press conference, on August 28, nearly one-third of the questions were related to Nixon's legal plight. If Ford wanted to move America forward, he would have to put Watergate behind him. On Sunday, September 8, 1974, President Ford, after taking the Holy Communion at St. John's Episcopal Church, in Washington, D.C., made a far less unifying surprise announcement than his amnesty program had proved to be. He appeared on national television that Sunday morning to tell the nation he was granting "a full, free and absolute pardon unto Richard Nixon for all offenses against the United States . . . he . . . may have committed."[11]

Ford's pardon decision was met with high-octane jeers. "The decision seemed baffling, shocking," Bob Woodward recalled. "Though there had been some published speculation that Ford would pardon Nixon, conventional wisdom, which I embraced, held that Nixon was radioactive."[12] Woodward — like many Americans — smelled a rat. He felt betrayed by Genial Jerry, the supposed exemplar of no-frills Midwestern straightforwardness. So too did his *Washington Post* colleague Carl Bernstein. The dreaded word "betrayal" was being bandied about Washington officialdom regarding Ford; it hung around the accidental president's neck with the finality of a tombstone salutation. Had Ford cut a quid pro quo agreement with Nixon (that is, resignation in exchange for pardon)? Why were the pardon terms so favorable to the ex-president? Did White House Chief of Staff Alexander Haig — the key link between Nixon and Ford — cut a deal between the two leaders? What legal information justified the pardon decision? Who advised Ford to make such a bold reversal? Questions like these rained down on Ford. Most reporters agreed with Woodward, who succinctly deemed the pardon "secret and dirty."

Ford may have shown mercy to Nixon, but the newspaper editorials were merciless on Ford. The *New York Times* claimed that this "blundering intervention" blow to the president's own cre Boston Globe chimed in that the "a gross misuse, if not abuse, of power." The *Washington Post* further, declaring that Ford's gr ___ ___ forgiveness was "nothing less than the continuation of a cover-up."[13] The conservative columnist George Will wrote: "The lethal fact is that Mr. Ford has now demonstrated that . . . he doesn't mean what he says."[14]

The first Gallup poll after the pardon reported that 59 percent of the public disapproved of it. The honeymoon was over. The historian Barry Werth, in his fine book *31 Days*, correctly deemed September 8 the "Day of the Avalanche." Hundreds of protest letters began piling up in the White House mailroom while the switchboard lighted up with calls running 8 to 1 against the pardon. The American Civil Liberties Union compared the pardon to the Nuremberg Trial "in which the Nazi leaders would have been let off." U.S. District Court Judge John Sirica, who had sent more than a dozen White House aides to prison, was livid over the pardon, later writing that if Nixon "had been convicted in my court, I would have sent him to jail."

The widespread suspicion that the pardon

...t of a secret deal between Nixon ...is handpicked successor irredeemably ...nished Gerald Ford's political career. Intended to put Watergate behind the nation once and for all, Ford's pardon of his predecessor did just the opposite in the minds of many Americans, who saw it as an extension of Nixon's unlamented "imperial presidency," stained with the same reliance on "executive privilege." *Washington Post* columnist Mary McGrory turned her trenchant pen on Ford, speaking for many in sneering, "He said he was 'healing the country.' What he was doing was a favor to an old friend while simultaneously trying to sink a nasty situation well before his own re-election campaign."[15]

In fact, the Nixon pardon should not have come as such a surprise. To begin with, Gerald Ford had never pretended to be anything but a pure politician, a profession in which long-term success depends on justifying the means with the ends. And in his very first remarks as president, "Our long national nightmare is over," he had made his desired end — a determination to leave Watergate (and, more to the point, Richard Nixon) in the past — clearly obvious.

What's more, speculation about a pardon for Nixon had begun almost a year before, at Ford's vice presidential confirmation hearings. There, on November 5, 1973, Ford had responded under questioning that he didn't think the public would stand for a president halting legal proceedings against a guilty predecessor. (And he was certainly right about that.) In the weeks after Nixon resigned, the debate flared up again. *Newsweek's* August 19 issue contained an analysis headlined "Should Nixon Be Granted Immunity?" in which it warned that a Ford pardon of Nixon would "smack too much of a deal between the two men."[16]

The matter appeared to have been put to rest by the end of August. Watergate special prosecutor Leon Jaworski resumed looking for ways to address the case against Nixon through judicial process. Jaworski later revealed that just before Nixon resigned, Haig had come to him to float the notion of terminating the case against the president once he forsook the nation's highest office. Jaworski was quick to add that Haig's gambit had failed, and no agreement concerning Nixon's fate had been reached with him. What gave the story significance was its revelation that Ford wasn't the only power broker Haig had approached to discern — or perhaps determine — Richard Nixon's fate.

For his part, Ford continued to deny that he had made any deal regarding Nixon's pardon, and a certain logic backed up his claims. By the time Haig called on Ford on August 1, Nixon's resignation was virtually assured, leaving his vice president no reason to negotiate. Ford was going to be his replacement; the only question was whether it would happen through Nixon's resignation or by his impeachment. If Ford promised him a pardon, the speculation went, Nixon would resign immediately; if not, the wounded president would drag the nation through a long and ugly impeachment process. The specter of such an arrangement came to haunt Ford from the moment he announced the pardon.

Deal or no deal, Richard Nixon never had much to fear from Gerald Ford, and he knew it. He had watched Ford prove his character through his twenty-six years in politics: aggressive with the strong but forgiving toward the weak, he may have been the least vindictive pol in Washington. Nixon also knew it was Ford's natural inclination to dispel trouble rather than prolong it; in fact, his antipathy for contention had guided many of his actions as House minority leader. In retrospect, even his antic defense of Nixon over the previous year looked like an attempt to schmooze the Watergate problem away. As vice president, Ford had made a point of keeping his distance from the scandal, so it hardly seemed likely that he would help let it fester on as president.

Given all he knew about Gerald Ford, it is a stretch to think that Richard Nixon truly feared that he would ever go to prison. He had picked his successor too well; a pardon of some sort was inevitable. Jerry Ford, his friend since 1949, wouldn't let him down. All that remained was the timing. And something, or several things, suddenly drove Ford to reverse his public stances on granting Nixon a pardon early in September.

According to Ford aide Robert Hartmann, the new president first mentioned the possibility of a pardon on August 30, when he told his most trusted advisers that he was tired of spending so much of his time addressing questions about Watergate. "Matter-of-factly," Hartmann recalled, "Ford said he was very much inclined to grant Nixon immunity from further persecution as soon as he was sure he had the legal authority to do so. There was a deafening silence. There is an antique clock on the Oval Office wall. . . . At this moment it shattered the silence like a burst of machine-gun fire."[17]

Philip Buchen, Ford's long-ago law partner, now serving as White House counsel, and his bright young colleague Benton Becker immediately set to poring over legal precedents regarding presidential pardons. Before long the pair produced a 1915 U.S. Supreme Court case, *Burdick v. United States,* that not only established that a pardon could be granted before any indictment had been handed down but that a pardon, once accepted, "carries an imputation of guilt, acceptance, a confession of it."[18]

In fact, the case had redefined the whole concept of a pardon. Issuing a pardon did not mean exoneration of the recipient, as most people thought. Instead, a pardon rendered a verdict without a trial — or punishment. Ford seized on the point. It just might be enough to make pardoning Nixon palatable. Thus the president wanted to make it clear to Nixon that if he accepted the pardon, he would in effect be admitting his guilt. To drive the point home, Becker was dispatched to San Clemente to go over all the ramifications of a pardon with Nixon in person.

As it turned out, Nixon already knew what Becker had come to tell him, just as he already knew what Ford was thinking at every step. Al Haig had been keeping his old boss informed of everything that was said in the supposedly confidential Oval Office discussions about a pardon for Nixon.[19] Ford should have known better than to trust his predecessor's take-charge chief of staff, but he couldn't grasp the level of deviousness Nixon had provoked in his staff. Gerald Ford's mistake lay in believing that his White House could operate according to his pledge of "candor and openness" when it remained packed with Nixon holdovers — a number of whom had at least as much reason to want Nixon pardoned immediately as the former president himself did.

For high-level Nixon associates such as Al Haig, Donald Rumsfeld, and Pat Buchanan — not to mention Henry Kissinger — a full-scale trial of the former chief executive posed many potential dangers. At best, such a proceeding would only further cement their ties to the nation's most scandal-mired administration; worse, a trial might open up new avenues of investigation these aides preferred to remain unexplored.

Among the more controversial aspects of the pardon Ford came to grant was that it did not cover those who had already been indicted for or convicted of Watergate-related crimes. Ironically, it would serve to protect those who had not yet been charged, however likely they were to be, as Nixon's pardon would effectively put an end to future Watergate investigations. Without Nixon, the impetus for further inquiries would simply lose steam. Knowing this, every White House holdover had good reason to root for Nixon's quick pardon, and those with influence over President Ford undoubtedly pushed the idea whenever they spoke with him.

In any event, during the first week of September, Ford certainly seemed in a rush to grant the pardon. He did so that weekend, without consulting any members of the House Judiciary Committee or Special Prosecutor Jaworski. Robert Hartmann suggested that Ford may have been warned by any number of intermediaries that Nixon's health was failing under the stress of his situation, or perhaps even that the disgraced ex-president was contemplating suicide. Those possibilities might indeed have accounted for the swiftness of Ford's action. On the morning of September 8, shortly before he informed the nation what he had done, Ford explained his decision to Jerald terHorst, who had just handed the president his letter of resignation over the pardon. "It was not an easy decision for me to make," Ford told his soon-to-be-ex-press secretary. "I thought about it a lot and prayed, too. . . . I'm not concerned about the election in 1976 or the politics of it. . . . I know there will be controversy over this, but it's the right thing to do and that's why I decided to do it now. I hope you can see that."[20]

Whether anyone could or not, once he announced Nixon's pardon on September 8, at least Ford knew his real work could finally begin. As he remarked later, "I felt I had come to the conclusion that I had an obligation — which was my own decision — to spend 100 percent of my time on the problems of 230 [*sic*] million people, rather than 25 percent of my time on the problems of one man."[21]

The pardon of Richard Nixon brought a quick end to the brief era of good feeling toward Jerry Ford. When Ford traveled to Pittsburgh the day after to deliver a speech on inflation, he was met by frenzied protestors chanting, "Jail Ford!" and one even waving a placard that read, "Up Yours!" The next afternoon the U.S. Senate passed a resolution by 55 to 24 urging Ford not to pardon anyone else associated with Watergate until the defendants had stood trial. The pardon was, simply put, bad politics. It was open season on Ford. Americans of every political stripe denounced the move with a vehemence that proved just how agonizing the Watergate crisis had been for the country — a new Gallup poll showed Ford's approval rating having instantly sunk from 71 to 50 percent.[22]

Ford's tenure abruptly entered its middle phase the day he pardoned Nixon. However controversial his choice may have been, and no matter how suspiciously rushed his announcement of it had seemed, the fact remained clear in Ford's mind that it had been his decision to make, and he stuck to it. A month later, the president took the near-unprecedented step of agreeing to appear at a public hearing for questioning by a House Judiciary subcommittee. During the two-hour hearing on October 17, broadcast live on national television, Ford repeated that he had granted the pardon "out of my concern to serve the best interests of my country." Although he revealed for the first time that he had discussed the possibility of a pardon with Al Haig a week before Nixon resigned, under harsh questioning Ford pounded the witness table and thundered back, "There was no deal, period."[23]

A year and a half later, Ford still stuck to his guns when asked about the Nixon pardon. "I did it, I did it at the right time and I am convinced that it was right," he replied. "I am convinced it was right in the national interest, and I would do it again."[24] In announcing the pardon, Ford had explained himself by asserting that the Nixon family's saga "is an American tragedy [and] someone must write and end to it. I have concluded that only I can do that. And if I can, I must. . . . As a man, my first consideration will always be to be true to my own convictions and my own conscience." Even veteran political reporters believed this, coming from Ford, and admired his steadfastness on the subject even if they despised his granting the pardon. Indeed, "no matter what the consequences," wrote Richard Reeves, "Gerald R. Ford, Jr., did it because of who he is — and he probably would have done it if he knew for certain it would destroy his Presidency."[25]

That rock-hard moral core defined Jerry Ford, as a man and as president. Ford's bedrock certainty of his own ethics enabled him to weather even the denunciation of most of his own countrymen. In fact, it was in that lonely moment after he pardoned Nixon to such a negative reaction that Ford seemed to rise to his new office for the first time. Unrattled by the speed of events or by their uneven consequences, Gerald Ford remained the steadiest of public men, certain of his course and confident in his ability to keep to it. He may have landed in the White House without planning to but he proved well prepared for the nation's highest office, intellectually as well as emotionally. In truth, if there was any artifice in Ford's approach to the presidency, it lay in his tendency to simplify himself and his ideas. On the personal front, his wife, Betty, was diagnosed with breast cancer in late September, leaving him in low spirits for months. But he never moped.[26] Unlike most statesmen, he consistently underplayed his own sophistication, or at least allowed others to. "Either by luck, happenstance, or divine grace," the historian Walter Isaacson summarized, "the nation's constitutional process had come forth with an unexpected president who was right for the moment."[27]

That said, Ford also understood that to be an effective president would take more than coming across as a regular Joe, welcome as the contrast was with Richard Nixon's arrogant aloofness. For all his colleagues' claims that the president remained the same good ol' Jerry Ford they had always known, it was by breaking with his

GOP partisan past that Ford would truly grow into the role of chief executive. As a member of Congress, Ford had rarely strayed from his beloved Republican Party's line. As House minority leader, he even more readily accepted the GOP's insistence on espousing only its partisan views. As Nixon's vice president he served much the same function, operating like a sort of Republican whip in the executive branch. As president, by contrast, Ford ignored his party's constraints to a surprising degree, becoming a far less political animal than at any other point in his long career.

He loosened his party ties deliberately, out of respect for his extraordinary position as the only U.S. president never to be elected to national office. Unlike all his predecessors (save George Washington), he had never slogged through the mud of a presidential campaign. Thus arriving in the White House with neither an untoward gratitude for those who had supported him nor any lingering animosity toward those who hadn't, Ford gained an unobstructed view of his enormous and widely diverse constituency. Outside the Fifth District of Michigan, he rarely encountered anyone who had ever voted for — or against — him. Ford fully grasped the special obligation this imposed on him, and felt honor bound to fulfill it.

Ford's record in the White House betrayed a remarkably evenhanded nonpartisanship regarding policies, as well as appointments. The onetime rock-solid conservative Republican chose as vice president the man who had given his name to the GOP's left-liberal wing, and he also brought a significant number of Democrats into his administration. Had Ford stayed closer to his roots instead of opting to forgo partisanship in favor of national unity, his party's conservative base might well have supported him. But at least he would leave the presidency in far better shape than he had found it, and perhaps even healthier than it had been in decades.

This feat appeared all the more impressive in light of the state of the nation whose leadership he had inherited. When Ford took over the presidency, *Congressional Quarterly* published a long list of the pressing issues facing him, including labor discontent, agriculture, commodity shortfalls, serious job losses in the housing industry, and many more — and that was just on the domestic side. Topping this dire agenda was a whole complex of troubles in the U.S. economy, which was not just ailing but ly-

his constituents to stop wasting so much food, pointing out the economic foolishness of buying more than they could eat and throwing the rest out. As sensible as Ford's 1974 economic initiative and the truths behind his speech were, unfortunately, the vast majority of Americans weren't buying it. They were too busy enjoying lower-priced gasoline, after the end of the Arab oil embargo of the previous winter. Sometime after World War II it seemed the nation had lost its capacity for self-sacrifice in the broader interest, no matter how worthy and smart the cause — and effects — might be. Thanks to this obtuseness, in late 1974 most Americans — including some of the president's own economic advisers — just laughed WIN off. Not surprisingly, Ford's well-intentioned appeal failed to put a dent in the country's economic problems.

Alongside the announcement of WIN on October 8, President Ford put forth a ten-point plan to right the U.S. economy. The centerpiece of the plan, a tax increase for corporations and high-income individuals, aimed to help control inflation while offsetting the deficit spending Nixon had bequeathed to his successor. Apart from its WIN component, the plan was largely the work of the Economic Policy Board, chaired by Secretary of the Treasury William Simon, a Nixon appointee and former Wall Street bond broker. As the newly created board's executive director, Ford recruited William Seidman, as a fellow Michigander who had made a fortune in the accounting business. The third member of Ford's economic troika, fiscal conservative Alan Greenspan, was a think-tank veteran whose nomination by Nixon to chair the Council of Economic Advisers made it through the Senate only after the presidency changed hands, becoming effective on September 1, 1974.

Another Nixon hand climbed to a higher rung under Ford later that month, but in this case by maneuvering out the ex-president's erstwhile right hand. Indeed, Donald Rumsfeld may have been the only operator in Washington savvy enough to get rid of Al Haig. Having evaded any connections to Watergate by taking the job of U.S. ambassador to NATO in February 1973, Rumsfeld returned from Europe to engineer himself back into the White House the old-fashioned, backroom way: by getting Haig kicked way upstairs and out of the country, to serve as supreme allied commander Europe as well as commander in chief of American forces in Europe — two military positions too prestigious to turn down.

With Haig out of the White House by the end of September 1974, Ford immediately boosted the overall efficiency of the operation, though in a style so combative it engendered internecine feuds that put those during the Nixon administration to shame. It would prove to be Rumsfeld who before long would see to the departures of both longtime Ford adviser Robert Hartmann and Secretary of Defense James Schlesinger, as well as the marginalization of Vice President Nelson Rockefeller and even superstar Secretary of State Henry Kissinger.

As his top deputy, Rumsfeld chose Dick Cheney, a self-effacing thirty-three-year-old from Wyoming who had been assisting Rumsfeld in various positions for several years. "Cheney's ascent in the Ford White House," James Mann averred in his book *The Rise of the Vulcans,* "served as an illustration of how an individual can rise to the top by virtue of his willingness to take care of the mundane chores that persons with larger egos avoid, thereby establishing reliability and learning all the inner workings of an organization."[31] The Ford White House's power-playing pair would quickly gain as much clout with their president as Haldeman and Ehrlichman had enjoyed with Nixon.

However efficiently his staff performed, nevertheless Gerald Ford found it hard to notch much progress. The president campaigned hard for Republican candidates in the November 1974 congressional elections, but with his administration's highlights to that point consisting of Nixon's pardon, the proposed tax hike, and WIN buttons, Ford proved of little help to his party. The Republicans lost five seats in the U.S. Senate and forty-eight in the House of Representatives. Although his career ambitions no longer hinged on the outcome, Ford still put enormous store in the midterm election results. He knew that without a congressional majority, his administration's ability to affect the legislative process would be hamstrung. Moreover, with Democrats holding enough votes to override a presidential veto, Ford knew that his chances of getting anything done through Congress would be slim.

What Ford realized, however, was that the midterm election wasn't just about the pardon. The public wanted government at all levels sanitized from Nixon contamination. When President Ford woke up on December 22, headed to Vail, Colorado, for Christmas, for example, he read an astounding *New York Times* story by investigative reporter Seymour Hersh, headlined "Huge CIA Operation Reported in U.S. Against Anti-War Forces." According to Hersh, the CIA had files on more than ten thousand Americans, filled with counterintelligence information garnered from illegal domestic wiretaps and postal snooping.[32]

Quickly Ford distanced himself from the CIA shenanigans. He had only been president for four months and knew nothing about CIA "watch lists" or spying on civil rights and peace activists traveling abroad. The only new Ford administration intelligence program was a heightened approach to dealing with "lost or stolen nuclear weapons and special nuclear materials, nuclear bomb threats, and radiation dispersal threats."[33] Nor did Ford know anything about the FBI bugging Martin Luther King Jr. or César Chávez.

But the *New York Times* revelations soon led to three investigations of domestic intelligence abuses. On January 4, 1975, Ford established the U.S. President's Commission on CIA Activities to investigate illegal surveillance by the CIA. (It became known as the Rockefeller Commission because it was chaired by the vice president.) Meanwhile, on January 27, the Senate created the Select Committee to Study Governmental

Operations with Respect to Intelligence Activities, chaired by Democratic senator Frank Church of Idaho, which became known as the Church Committee. A few weeks later, the House launched an investigation into CIA expenditures and effectiveness. All three created a media sensation. Stories appeared about the CIA trying to assassinate foreign leaders, including Cuba's Fidel Castro and the Dominican Republic's Rafael Trujillo. Astutely, Ford distanced himself from the revelations, making sure he wasn't tainted by the misdeeds from the Kennedy, Johnson, and Nixon administrations. The Rockefeller and Church investigations, for Ford, were lessons on how he didn't want to operate as president. He returned the country to more traditional Cold War policies, working through NATO and promoting the burgeoning European Community.[34]

7

THE AGONY OF PEACE

Predictably, many leading Democrats lambasted Ford's pardon of Richard Nixon as rank corruption. Leading the charge was Senator Edward Kennedy of Massachusetts, who painted the pardon as an unforgivable "betrayal of the public trust."[1] Politically speaking, however, the pardon was a gift to the Democratic Party. After the Democrats swept the midterm election in 1974, Republicans focused their ire on Gerald Ford. House Minority Leader John Rhodes of Ohio, for example, blamed the pardon for the November rout.[2] Senator Barry Goldwater had warned Ford about the deleterious consequences of handing Nixon a "Get Out of Jail Free" pass. "It doesn't make any sense," Goldwater had told Ford on September 8, insisting that Nixon go to trial. "He may be clear in your eyes, but he's not clear in mine."[3]

With the midterm election over, the Republican Right, led by Goldwater, did everything it could to distance itself from Ford. Conservatives did not want the "accidental president" to be their party's candidate in 1976. Immediately following the election, Ronald Reagan, flush with ambition, publicly distanced himself from Ford in his weekly newspaper column and radio address. It was a signal of things to come. "When I interviewed Reagan in the fall of 1974," the journalist Lou Cannon recalled, "he said nothing positive about Ford and claimed it was too early to judge his administration."[4] Conservatives now saw Ford as the quasi-enemy.

Among the tactics President Ford picked up from his predecessor was Nixon's way of dealing with rancor at home: to go abroad. So with the U.S. economy still troubled in late November 1974, and the midterm election a GOP disaster, Ford left on a tour of Asian nations, including Japan (the first time ever for a U.S. president) and South Korea. His last stop was Vladivostok, the Soviet Union's Asiatic port city, where he was to meet with Soviet leader Leonid Brezhnev. Ford arrived for a round of serious talks, but was delighted to find that the friendly Brezhnev shared his good-natured sense of humor. "Both were rugged outdoor men of action," recalled Bill Hyland, an American delegate. "They loved sports and good stories, and in other times or in other places they may have become genuinely friendly."[5]

The purpose of the meeting was no laughing matter: to consider extending the 1972 Strategic Arms Limitation Talks (SALT I) agreement. Many Cold War hard-liners, Democrats as well as Republicans, opposed even exploring a SALT II treaty on the grounds that the United States had everything to lose, having developed very different weapons systems from the Soviet Union's arsenal. The presumption held that a new arms-limitation treaty would unfairly restrain the U.S. missile program, which focused on precisely targeted light warheads, while likely leaving the USSR its full complement of much heavier warheads on larger missiles. The whole idea of détente, the Cold War thaw initiated by Nixon and Kissinger in 1972, had grown unpopular with many in Congress, who felt that the improvement in U.S.-Soviet relations had been gained at the cost of a naïve accommodation to the Communists' underlying expansionist aims.

When he arrived in Vladivostok, Gerald Ford may have been new to the execution of foreign policy, though not strictly speaking to the practice of diplomacy. Over his quarter century in the House he'd engaged in any number of tough negotiations, with both allies and opponents at least as intransigent as any foreign leader. Although Brezhnev was more vehement and intractable than most, Ford nonetheless held firm regarding the equation for balancing the two nations' missile capabilities. The U.S.-backed formula did not lay the "symmetrical" groundwork Kissinger had favored but instead held the Soviets to an even tighter definition of "equality" in number of weapons, regardless of their size or type. Yet, in the end, the bargaining session was successful, and the Soviets were more accommodating than Ford had imagined.

Ford felt pleased and optimistic about leaving Vladivostok with a framework for a SALT II treaty. "The American people would be delighted to hear that my meeting with Brezhnev had gone so well," he recalled thinking at the time, "and Congress, with some exceptions, would probably endorse the new accord."[6] The president was proved wrong on both counts. Senator Henry "Scoop" Jackson, a Cold War hawk, led a crusade to derail SALT II, believing the Vladivostok framework was riddled with holes. Chief among Jackson's concerns was that the Kremlin wasn't including the Backfire bomber in the deal, and that the United States needed to take the new Tomahawk air-launched cruise missiles off the table. The deficiencies with SALT II were, in the words of Walter Isaacson, "the devils that resided in its unfinished details."[7] Many Americans also resented that, as the U.S. economy sputtered, their chief executive left his watch to share vodka toasts with the country's sworn adversary as well as dubious allies such as the Japanese, whose inexpensive imports were making aggressive inroads into the American auto market. "The criticism of détente, by both Jackson and Reagan, was done for political reasons," Kissinger later complained. "And that upsets me. It meant we couldn't do what we should have done on arms control."[8]

But America's economic woes were very real. That December, when the U.S. unemployment rate reached 6.5 percent, Ford had no choice but to invoke the dreaded word "recession" and to admit that nearly every major economic indicator was headed in the wrong direction. Ever mindful of, if not driven by, public opinion, the president immediately dedicated himself to tending to the economy first and foremost, and would keep it his administration's priority. Although many began to wonder whether Ford had the mettle to tackle the nation's complex financial problems, he was actually quite up to the task. According to the historian John Robert Greene, Ford, perhaps due to his long service on the House Appropriations Committee, "understood the intricacies of economics and economics policy better than any president of the twentieth century."[9]

Unfortunately, Ford's grasp of the situation by January 1975 would directly contradict his understanding of it just three months earlier. Rather than go through with the $5 billion tax hike he had announced in October, Ford unveiled a new economic strategy centered around cutting taxes for most individuals and businesses while levying a windfall tax on oil refineries — which had been profiting enormously from the very shortages strangling the rest of the economy. Conservatives, including Treasury Secretary Simon, bristled at the president's turn from the battle against inflation to combat the recession on another front. By their thinking, a recession would right itself eventually, whereas inflation opened a gaping wound that would bleed the life out of any economy if left unstanched. Ford chose the counsel of more moderate advisers such as Bill Seidman and Alan Greenspan, who maintained that sophisticated methods to curb inflation should be applied later, because it was the recession that was doing the most immediate harm to the country.

Stung by accusations from all sides that he had flip-flopped on how best to address the nation's economic crisis, President Ford learned fast just how lonely the middle ground can be. Already decried by conservatives for its potential to send the federal budget deficit and interest rates soaring, the "reasonable" tax cut Ford had proposed ballooned over eleven weeks of debate in Congress from $16 billion to $24.8 billion.[10] Even then, most Democrats weren't satisfied with the size of the tax cuts — nor with Ford's accompanying proposal to hold the line on any new federal spending programs other than energy projects. Yet there was more to the legislative impasse than that. In the early months of 1975, the overwhelmingly Democratic Ninety-fourth Congress worked against not only the president as a Republican but also the very prerogatives of the executive branch that Richard Nixon had lately exploited. In any case, most congressional Democrats saw no reason to cooperate with Gerald Ford: they controlled the Senate by 61 to 39 and the House by 291 to 144. So, as dead set against government expansion as he had been through his entire career, Ford found himself with no choice but to sign an economic relief package festooned with new federal programs aimed at providing just that by creating new jobs.

As was his wont, Ford responded to his opponents' challenge by devising a game plan to win them over toward his goals. He had picked up some extra yardage late in 1974 by sacking more Nixon holdovers, most notably in the Watergate-roiled Justice Department, which had been headed by four different attorneys general in less than two and a half years. When the controversy-prone William B. Saxbe became the first member of Ford's cabinet to resign, on December 18, 1974, the president saw a chance to make a point with his choice of replacement.

More than any other arm of the executive branch, the Department of Justice had been politicized top to bottom by previous administrations, culminating with Nixon's use of it as an extension of his reelection campaign. On principle (as well as with an eye toward appeasing Congress), Ford determined to draw his new attorney general from outside the political, or even public, arena. Chief of Staff Rumsfeld suggested the legal scholar Edward H. Levi, the president of the University of Chicago. Ford found Levi's credentials impressive and his standing as a progressive with a predilection for law and order ideal. At first the president had a hard time securing support for the nomination from right-leaning senators who assumed that, coming from academia, Levi must be a liberal. Ford's commitment to depoliticizing the justice system didn't end with Levi's confirmation, however. His administration would continually ignore the usual partisan priorities in filling federal judgeships.

"Rather than imposing ideological considerations or its own legal-policy goals," explained the scholar David M. O'Brien, "Ford's Department of Justice sought high-caliber nominees."[11] However well intended, the gambit would contribute greatly to the president's loss of backing within his own party. Reagan administration official Stephen Markman would articulate the GOP view years later: "The weakness of the Ford Administration may be seen in the statistic that a record 21 percent of its district court appointments went to members of the opposing party."[12]

Of course, the Democrats' sweeping gains in the 1974 congressional elections may have had something to do with Ford's new embrace of nonpartisanship. The Republicans' staggering losses left the president little choice but to aggressively appease the opposition if he wanted to get anything done. And the only thing that would appease them was an end to the Vietnam War.

To that point, of course, the United States had never lost a war, and many Americans would rather have been damned than see it lose this one in Southeast Asia. But not losing didn't necessarily require winning — or even ending the conflict. Officially, the Korean conflict still went on, albeit locked in the stalemate mandated by the compromise that suspended the fighting in 1953. The Paris Peace Talks had left the Vietnam War similarly unresolved. The negotiations' much-heralded peace agreement rested on the cessation of offensives by North Vietnam along with the withdrawal of all U.S. combatants. While the Paris accords spelled out the requisite completeness of the latter, however, they failed to address the consequences should the North Vietnamese resume aggression against the South. According to the agreement worked out in January 1973, henceforth the United States could protect its ally only through continuing financial aid.

North Vietnamese negotiator Le Duc Tho and U.S. secretary of state Henry Kissinger were jointly awarded the 1973 Nobel Peace Prize for their efforts to forge the Paris accords. Perhaps out of conscience, Le Duc Tho declined his share in the prize. Peace, it turned out, was not his goal. He had correctly calculated that once the Americans were out of Vietnam, they would have little stomach for returning, no matter what. Indeed, the U.S. Congress made no secret of that fact, reducing aid to South Vietnam by half for 1973 and then by half again for the year after. In August 1974, however, the situation seemed susceptible to change as the supposedly hawkish Gerald Ford took over the presidency. He even lived up to the image by closing his very first day in the White House by meeting with Graham Martin, the U.S. ambassador to South Vietnam. Hanoi would be watching, as Ford well knew.

Hanoi was also watching, however, when the Democrats triumphed in that November's congressional elections. Many of them had won by campaigning against everything Richard Nixon had stood for, including "peace with honor" in Vietnam. And even before they were seated, ever more moderates and even some conservatives began joining the newly elected liberals in calling for an end to the whole bloody mess in Southeast Asia. This conflict, the longest war in American history, had also grown into its most expensive, having cost some $150 billion by 1974. With so little return, it was no wonder the citizenry elected so many representatives pledged to cutting the nation's losses by just pulling out.

That December, the outgoing Ninety-third Congress overwhelmingly approved a Foreign Assistance Act that reduced the appropriation for South Vietnam. Ford held out hope that the cuts might be restored in a supplemental grant, as congressional leaders promised to consider later, if need be. The North Vietnamese, however, proved less inclined to wait. Having poked at South Vietnam's perimeter for more than a year in contravention of the Paris accords, the Communists launched a major New Year offensive against America's ally. On January 6, 1975, North Vietnamese forces captured the Southern provincial capital of Phuoc Binh. According to Henry Kissinger, "Phuoc Binh was the test case. If the United States reacted, there was still a chance for Hanoi to withdraw from the brink."[13] But the United States did nothing.

Gerald Ford's natural inclination was to protect the South Vietnamese, at the very least by sending aid. "With adequate United States military assistance, they can hold their own," he proclaimed.[14] Whether or not that was true, by law Ford could do very little to prove his point. Since the end of World War II, Congress had seen how presidents could let just such military assistance lead into major wars, declared or otherwise. By the time Ford sat in the Oval Office, the legislature had the chief executive on a much shorter leash. As passed by Congress over Nixon's veto in November 1973, the War Powers Act held the president's authority to commit U.S. troops to combat abroad without congressional approval for only sixty days. Thus, despite the increasingly aggressive Communist pressure on South Vietnam in January 1975, Ford could do little but keep negotiating — and begging for aid money from Congress.

Hanoi's leaders took full advantage of Ford's predicament. Emboldened by the political restraints on the U.S. president, they continued stepping up military action on the ground. They grew so self-assured, in fact, that North Vietnamese premier Pham Van Dong sneered that "even if we offered the Americans a bribe to intervene again, they would not accept it."[15] Ignoring every dictate of the Paris Peace Accords, the Communist leaders in Hanoi formulated plans to take Saigon in 1976, perhaps 1977. They would beat both deadlines.

Under the North's continuing and concerted attacks, the South Vietnamese began withdrawing into Saigon, their own capital, early in 1975. The unruliness of their retreat only doomed their fortunes faster. Soldiers and civilians alike abandoned their country's northern provinces in panic, needlessly ceding strategic strongholds and leaving behind valuable matériel. The wasteful haste came, of course, from fear — but not just of the approaching North Vietnamese troops. The terror also sprang from the sudden absence of American support. The Communists, after all, had been in the South Vietnamese countryside for a generation. Now for the first time in all those years, U.S. help was not forthcoming. Although South Vietnam's leaders kept expecting their superpower ally to intervene again, their people seemed to know better, and the resulting panic devolved into utter chaos.

According to Robert Hartmann, Ford had considered the situation in South Vietnam hopeless since 1967, when President

Johnson had restricted bombing of the North, effectively ensuring that the United States would wage only a large-scale war — not an all-out one.[16] As commander in chief, Ford maintained that even though the war was South Vietnam's to win or lose, the United States remained responsible for its longtime ally's ability to put up a fight for its freedom. He said so often, with Congress generally ignoring him and South Vietnamese president Nguyen Van Thieu hanging on his every word. Thieu felt certain that Ford's steady rhetoric held the promise of renewed American intervention. He believed he had good reason to think so: a written promise from Ford's predecessor. In secret correspondence, most notably in the autumn of 1972 during the Paris Peace Talks, Nixon had gone out of his way to assure Thieu that he could sign the forthcoming accords with the utmost confidence that the U.S. government would stand by him should the peace collapse. Like a car salesman trying to clinch a deal on a lemon, Nixon had repeated these assurances to his skittish client again and again. On January 17, 1973, for instance, Nixon sent Thieu another secret letter in which he stated unequivocally, "First, we recognize your Government as the sole legitimate Government of South Vietnam; Secondly, we do not recognize the right of foreign troops to remain on South Vietnamese soil; Thirdly, the U.S. will react vigorously to violations of the Agreement."[17]

The same pledges did not, of course, appear in the Paris Peace Accords. The problem with the Nixon letters, which could have been seen to constitute a corollary to the accords — and, to Thieu's mind, even to supersede the agreement — was that no one in either Congress or the State Department had ever seen them, which nullified their serving as official instruments of U.S. diplomacy. Nonetheless, Thieu kept Nixon's secret letters in a bundle in his bedroom dresser drawer.[18] To him, they guaranteed South Vietnam's continued independence despite the imminent threat form the North. But Richard Nixon was back stewing in Southern California for good, leaving it largely up to Gerald Ford to determine just exactly what the correspondence meant.

When the Nixon letters' existence became known early in April 1975, courtesy of Thieu's administration, Ford claimed that he had not yet read them all. It was not, of course, the first time he had chosen to remain ignorant of the specifics of something Nixon had hatched, so as not to have to lie about it. Ford took the position that the letters must have only reiterated the tenets of the Paris Peace Accords, although Nixon's promises actually went much further in committing the United States to intervene in the event of proscribed Communist aggression. Various members of Congress spoke out immediately to denounce and discredit the letters, partly to protect their new prerogatives under the War Powers Act. No matter how Ford may have felt personally about America's obligation to South Vietnam, he made it perfectly clear that his White House wasn't duty bound to act in line with another of Nixon's under-the-table schemes.

Through the winter of 1974–75, Ford made one last push to drum up financial support for South Vietnam via public appearances and appeals to Congress. The effort proved fruitless. Among his top advisers only Kissinger kept pressing for continuing aid to the South Vietnamese, and the feeling in some quarters was that Kissinger was only trying to protect his reputation by shifting the blame for the failed peace onto Congress. No one would have put it past him, but the secretary of state wasn't alone in his multilayered motivations. Ford surely waged his campaign for aid to South Vietnam knowing full well that success would mean the United States would continue to prop up Thieu's government with supplies, and perhaps even more American lives — and that the Vietnam War would go on. And with that, Ford's presidency would be sucked all the way into the quagmire that had maimed both the Johnson and the Nixon administrations. But knowing that Congress wouldn't budge, Ford could speak out on behalf of South Vietnam, preserving America's (as well as his own) honor and still not lengthen the war. Had Congress been more compliant, one can only wonder whether Ford would have taken the same course.

As it was, in March the North Vietnamese took control of fifteen more Southern provinces, including Darlac, Pleiku, and Kontum. "My guess," remarked one Western diplomat, "is that a lot of Communist generals are wondering what they did right for a change."[19] Whatever that was, unless the situation changed immediately, nothing would stop their advance.

To see what could, Ford dispatched a fact-finding delegation to Saigon. Its leader, U.S. Army chief of staff General Frederick C. Weyand, reported on April 5 that it would cost roughly $722 million just to secure a defense perimeter around Saigon. In other words, three-quarters of a billion dollars would buy the United States enough time to ensure the safe exit of its citizens from its doomed Indochinese ally.

Official White House photographer David Hume Kennerly, who had accompanied the delegation to Saigon, returned with a more candid report to the president. "I don't care what the generals tell you," Kennerly blurted with the bluntness Ford valued him for. "They're bullshitting you if they say that Vietnam has got more than three or four weeks left. There's no question about it. It's just not gonna last."[20]

Ford no longer had any reason to believe otherwise. On April 21, President Thieu resigned his office, made a speech accusing the United States of selling South Vietnam out to the Communists, and fled to Switzerland.[21] Ford duly requested the $722 million from Congress to protect Saigon's new caretaker government, but he had already decided what to do regarding Vietnam. And once Gerald Ford made a decision, he acted on it. In an April 23 speech before six thousand Tulane University students jammed into the basketball field house, he declared: "Today, America can regain the sense of pride that existed before Vietnam.

But it cannot be achieved by refighting a war that is finished as far as America is concerned."[22]

The Tulane students cheered wildly as if the home team had just won a game. The Vietnam War was "finished." The president had said so. The paroxysms of whooping were so sustained it took even Ford by surprise. The bleachers rocked.[23] The Associated Press fired off a bulletin announcing that an era of American history had ended. The very same day, a Gallup poll showed that 78 percent of the American public opposed further U.S. aid to support South Vietnam, with only 17 percent favoring the outlay and 5 percent expressing no opinion.[24] The war was indeed already over as far as most of the American people were concerned. What made Ford's April 23 speech significant was its revelation that their commander in chief finally agreed. For the first time in decades, the public and their president were on the same wavelength on Vietnam.

When the applause at last died down in New Orleans, Ford continued on a more somber but equally pragmatic note. "We are, of course, saddened indeed by the events in Indochina. Events, tragic as they are, [that] portend neither the end of the world nor of America's leadership in the world."[25]

How Jerry Ford had changed. With his speech at Tulane, the erstwhile internationalist made it clear that he would not put the United States through any more pain for the sake of South Vietnam. What's more, the once-dependable Cold War hawk declared there was no shame in walking off without a victory, at least from this long and ugly war. In truth, Ford's acceptance of the inevitable collapse of two longtime U.S. allies — for Cambodia was falling to the Communists that spring as well — proved a defining moment for both his administration and his character. "I am determined as a president can be to seek national rediscovery of the belief in ourselves," he explained. "I ask that we stop fighting the battles and the recriminations of the past. I ask that we look now at what is right with America."[26]

It was the same desire for renewal that had prompted Ford to pardon Richard Nixon. Like that risky decision, his move to pull America out of Vietnam grew from his expedient belief in facing the inevitable sooner rather than later. In both instances, Ford opted to make the hard choices fast. After the slow agonies that Watergate and Vietnam had put the nation through, seizing the first opportunities to move on from them just seemed the sensible thing to do.

At the same time, Ford's remarks at Tulane were deemed a slap at Henry Kissinger, who had not been informed beforehand that the president was about to declare the war "finished." Naturally, the secretary of state was less than pleased to be blindsided by Ford's April 23 proclamation, even if he did understand the predicament of this "strong, honorable and genuinely decent man," as he would describe Gerald Ford in his memoirs.[27] Although Kissinger had long spearheaded the nation's unsuccessful diplomatic efforts to end the war less than a month before, on March 27, he had in effect given the president his blessing to abandon the war. Nearly three decades later Kissinger would recall telling Ford at that White House meeting, "Maybe you must put Vietnam behind you and not tear the country apart again."[28] Kissinger, in other words, agreed that the war was over. What he objected to was being blackballed from the decision-making process, which culminated in New Orleans. "The line about the war being finished — Henry didn't like that sentence," Ford later noted. "I knew he wanted to keep fighting for more aid and that he blamed Congress. And I did, too.

But having been up there on the Hill for twenty-five years, I just didn't think it would be all that productive to give them unshirted hell. That's where Henry and I disagreed. And I was right. I understood the system better."[29]

Suddenly, all that remained of America's longest and most divisive military conflict was the urgent need to evacuate the approximately six thousand U.S. citizens still in South Vietnam — a number that swelled by sixfold when the Americans' Vietnamese wives, children, and in-laws wanted out, too. President Ford was nearly as concerned for the safety of the tens of thousands of South Vietnamese who had openly sided with the United States, and even for those who just pretended to as the Communists closed on the gates of the capital city. Ever forgiving, Ford pledged not to turn anyone away. Instead, he approved a massive exodus program that flew some forty thousand Americans and Vietnamese out from the Saigon airport. After that, enemy fire on the outgoing planes, although it inflicted no casualties, forced the evacuation to switch to helicopters shuttling off the roof of the U.S. embassy to a waiting fleet of navy ships massed off the coast. Some 1,737 Americans and 5,680 Vietnamese were choppered off the embassy roof in that chaotic last week of April 1975, during which the U.S. Navy ships rescued another thirty-two thousand Vietnamese who had fled the Communists by sea in tiny boats.

Throughout the harrowing mass escape, Ford held firm to his promise that all the South Vietnamese who managed to get out could find a new home in the United States. Not all of his countrymen shared that magnanimous view, but Ford wouldn't budge. As he saw it, embracing the democratically inclined citizens of Vietnam was the least America could do for these allies. Indeed, he welcomed some of the refugees to San Francisco personally. "As the clock ran down on resistance in Saigon," Robert Hartmann wrote later, "I watched the President move calmly and confidently through the evacuation minefield. . . . When the lives of multitudes and the international image of America hung in the balance, Ford acted as if he'd been President all of his life."[30]

Declassified documents from this period give factual credence to Hartmann's claim. As noted in late March 1975, President Ford had sent General Weyand to Saigon to assess the situation and bring back a full report with recommendations. The most compelling product of the Weyand mission came from Kenneth M. Quinn, a National Security Council adviser on East Asia who, on April 5, wrote Kissinger a private ten-page memorandum so bleak it stands as the grimmest and most accurate assessment by the Ford administration of America's final weeks in South Vietnam. The South Vietnamese forces "may be totally defeated in as little as three weeks," Quinn noted. "President Thieu is discredited and almost completely ineffective. He can no longer provide the leadership necessary to rally the country. The morale of the army and civilian population is critically low and bordering on national despair. Fear of the communists is widespread, and people from all walks of life are now searching for a way to flee the country. Panic is seemingly just below the surface, and an imminent attack on Saigon could lose it [for us]."[31]

Just five days after the Quinn report, Ford went hat in hand before a joint session of Congress to request $722 million in emergency military aid plus $250 million for economic and humanitarian assistance for the people of South Vietnam. "The options before us are few, and the time is short," the president pleaded. "We cannot . . . abandon our friends." The Senate Armed

Services Committee disagreed, and on April 17 rejected the appeal, causing the genial Ford to pound his fist and exclaim, "Those bastards." Meanwhile, Kissinger, in an April 24 State Department meeting, was reduced to denouncing those "treacherous bastards in France" who seemed hell-bent on celebrating America's misadventure in Southeast Asia. What the Ford Library's documents show, however, is that neither the president nor Kissinger ever really thought Congress would appropriate more money; the nearly billion-dollar request was largely a ruse to buy more time to plan for the imminent evacuation of Saigon and to pin Congress with the historical blame for losing Vietnam.

Another debate was shaping up behind closed doors. On the same day the Senate committee rejected Ford's proposal, Kissinger cabled Ambassador Martin: "We have just completed an interagency review of the State of Play in South Vietnam. You should know that at the emergency White House meeting today there was almost no support for the evacuation of Vietnamese or for the use of American force to help protect any evacuation. The sentiment of our military, DOD and CIA colleagues was to get out fast and now."[32] But the declassified record also shows that the commander in chief insisted that the United States had a moral and humanitarian obligation to airlift out as many South Vietnamese as possible and bring them to America. At Ford's behest, Kissinger cabled Martin on April 24. "We are amazed at the small number of Vietnamese being evacuated, considering the substantial amount of aircraft available," he wrote. "I know you feel, as we do, a heavy moral obligation to evacuate as many deserving Vietnamese as possible, and I urge you to redouble your efforts in that regard. The President expects these instructions to be carried out fully and within the time schedule he has set out. For his part, he plans to call the NSC together this afternoon to lay down the law."[33]

Some of the most compelling reading in the Ford Library on the final days of U.S. military involvement in Vietnam comes from the more than one hundred transcribed pages of authorized National Security Agency intercepts of helicopter radio messages sent during the frantic evacuation of the U.S. embassy in Saigon on April 29, 1975. Operation Frequent Wind, as the rescue mission was dubbed, takes on a dramatic new immediacy in the words of the pilots dodging mortar fire and gas bombs to save U.S. embassy staff members before attempting to rescue any South Vietnamese. "Reports are that there are 200 Americans left to evacuate," an intercept reads. "Gunners Six to GSF Commander. Bring personnel up through the building. Do not let them [the South Vietnamese] follow too closely. Use Mace if necessary, but do not fire on them."[34] Despite firefights around the building, Ambassador Martin, the other remaining Americans, and the luckiest South Vietnamese nationals climbed the ladder and made it out safely to the United States. "The ladder was seen by everybody else as the symbol of our failure in Vietnam," Ford later recalled. "But, being an optimist, I saw it as a symbol of freedom. Fred and Frank Meijer, both friends, eventually helped me bring that ladder back to the United States. They stood up against Henry [Kissinger] on that one, and won."[35]

The owners of a chain of supercenters in Michigan would hardly seem a match for Henry Kissinger in a debate over the Vietnam War, but at the 1995 board meeting of the Gerald R. Ford Foundation, the former secretary of state indeed lost a heated argument on the subject to Fred Meijer of Grand Rapids. At issue was an eighteen-step metal ladder, utterly unremarkable except that in April 1975 thousands of desperate South Vietnamese, fleeing capture by the invading North Vietnamese for freedom in the United States, had clambered up its sturdy steps onto the roof of the U.S. embassy in Saigon and into American helicopters perched there. To Meijer, the gray ladder was an uplifting symbol of hope; to Kissinger, it was a grim reminder of the U.S. failure in South Vietnam that had cost more than fifty-eight thousand American lives.

It was Meijer's entrepreneurial son Hank who unwittingly sparked the contention when he went to Ho Chi Minh City (formerly Saigon) in October 1994, in search of promising new business ventures that might result from the Clinton administration's impending normalization of relations with Vietnam. While driving down Le Duan Boulevard one afternoon, Hank Meijer asked his driver to stop at the former U.S. embassy, atop which the tragic last moments of America's involvement in Vietnam had been played out. Abandoned and allowed to be run down into a weed-choked eyesore where only chickens wandered among the shards of broken glass, the padlocked building was slated for the wrecking ball.

"Then I saw the ladder from the evacuation," Hank Meijer relates. "My first thought was, 'That's an important piece of history; perhaps I can pay somebody a few hundred bucks to weld it off with a blowtorch, then crate it up and ship it back to Michigan for display at the Ford Museum.' " When he returned to Grand Rapids and told his father, Fred Meijer, about the ladder, the elder Mejier was captivated, and determined to put those "eighteen steps to freedom" on permanent display before the American people. He figured his fellow board members at the foundation would agree — but when he broached the idea of acquiring the ladder at the next meeting he met with surprisingly harsh resistance from Kissinger. "It's just a terrible idea," the nation's only celebrity diplomat kept repeating. "Why would you want to remind visitors about this horrible chapter in American history?"

Somewhat startled, Meijer held his ground. "Henry, if we don't acquire the ladder, it will end up in the bowels of the Smithsonian." To which an annoyed Kissinger shot back, "That's a good place for it."[36]

Then the ex-president spoke up, likening the "freedom ladder" to the concrete slab from the Berlin Wall that adorns the museum's entrance. "No one knows more than I how humiliating it was," Ford reminded his secretary of state. "As you recall, I had to sit in the Oval Office and watch our troops get kicked out of Vietnam. But it's part of our history, and we can't forget it." The decision was made to get the ladder. "To some, this staircase will always be seen as an emblem of military defeat," Ford noted. "For me, however, it symbolizes man's undying desire to be free."[37]

8
THE *Mayaguez*
INCIDENT AND THE
HELSINKI ACCORDS

America's only unelected president did what his four predecessors could not: he extricated the United States from Vietnam's long-running civil war. Yet even though that was what most of his constituents wanted, and despite the final U.S. evacuation from Saigon having gone better "than we had any right to expect," as the commander in chief himself put it, Gerald Ford got only mixed reviews for ending America's part in the conflict. The lack of acclaim drew in part from what Ford's achievement revealed: that U.S. involvement in Indochina had accomplished little, and at high cost. "If we had pulled out ten years ago, Viet Nam would have fallen then," summed up Harold Hannon, a U.S. Army officer who had been deployed to the embattled country during the Eisenhower presidency, with the small first wave of American advisers. "If we had stayed on another ten years, they still would have collapsed when we pulled out. This is a battle we lost. You can't win them all." But before Vietnam, America *had* won them all. And therein lay the problem with Jerry Ford, in the eyes of some of his countrymen.

The message the Ford evacuation gave was hard to swallow: that it had been for nothing that 8.75 million Americans had served, that 154,000 had been seriously wounded, and that more than 58,000 had died. Even worse, to the hawkish, was the resulting perception that the richest and supposedly mightiest superpower in the world had been humiliated by a ragtag band of Third World guerrillas. As simplistic and ethnocentric as that may have been — Ho Chi Minh and his North Vietnamese followers had demonstrated the power of nationalism in their decades-long struggle against the French and the Americans — the image lingered that the United States had become the "pitiful, helpless giant" Nixon had warned about five years earlier.[1]

Fortuitously, events didn't leave America looking weak for long. Just twelve days after the fall of Saigon, Indochina was the site of another challenge to American power. On May 12, 1975, a Cambodian patrol boat seized the *Mayaguez,* a U.S. merchant ship,

185

and its crew of thirty-nine for allegedly entering territorial waters in the Gulf of Siam. What turned this incident into a crisis was the overheated U.S. response to it, which would cost forty-one American, and many more Cambodian, lives. The 480-foot container ship carried either "a cargo of U.S. government materiel," according to the antiwar journalist William Shawcross,[2] or "a cargo of food, paints and chemicals," according to Gerald Ford.[3]

In any case, the *Mayaguez* was about sixty miles off the Cambodian coast — but only six to eight miles from the tiny isle of Poulo Wai, then being warred over by the Communist governments of Cambodia and Vietnam — when it radioed a distress call: "Have been fired upon and boarded by Cambodian armed forces."

Although initial intelligence reports wrongly stated that the *Mayaguez* had been forced to the mainland port of Kompong Som, it had been held near where it was captured for some twelve hours before being supposedly escorted to the Cambodian island of Koh Tang, thirty-four miles off the coast. (It was later revealed that the *Mayaguez* was actually taken to the island of Rong Sam Lem.) As it turned out, at least to that juncture, the worrisome situation

186

aboard the ship had stayed surprisingly benign. According to the *Mayaguez* crew, in fact, their Cambodian captors didn't even try to seem threatening. "They were a raggedy bunch and they didn't know how to use things," one of the U.S. merchant seamen recalled. "The shower was a big hit. Once we showed them how to use it, they had a ball. One guy held the gun and the rest piled in under the shower." The American sailors described their treatment as astonishingly polite. "At first I thought the Cambodians were going to take us out and shoot us," another crewman said later, "but they were so nice, really kind. They fed us first and everything. I hope everybody gets hijacked by them."[4]

Things weren't nearly as calm at the White House, where officials essentially had no idea what was going on in the Gulf of Siam. The uncertainty spawned antsy memories of the USS *Pueblo,* a navy intelligence ship the North Koreans had seized in 1968. Then, eighty-two American sailors had been imprisoned for eleven months before the Johnson administration admitted to a territorial-waters violation to secure their release. No one in the Ford administration wanted to replay that embarrassment born of reluctance to use armed force. What's more, no one in the White House thought it wise to assume anything but the worst about the Khmer Rouge Communists who had taken over Cambodia less than a month before. The Khmer Rouge, headed by Pol Pot, had launched a horrific wave of genocide and repression. "Foreign policy considerations weighed heavily as well," Henry Kissinger would admit in his third volume of memoirs. "Especially in the aftermath of Indochina's collapse, the United States needed to demonstrate that there were limits to what it would tolerate."[5]

With the last consideration apparently uppermost, President Ford consulted with his full range of cabinet, military, diplomatic, and political advisers, and then ordered a considerable force of U.S. ships, aircraft, and 1,100 marines to the region. During the two days it would take them to get there, Ford instructed Kissinger to work on a diplomatic solution. The secretary of state, who was pushing the hardest for a strong military response, delegated the gentler approach to the chief of the U.S. Liaison Office in Beijing, George H. W. Bush. Try as he did, Bush couldn't get far, because even his network of Asian contacts didn't know whom to talk to in the new Cambodian government.

As the prevailing confusion continued, the imperative remained to get the *Mayaguez*'s thirty-nine crewmen out of Cambodian hands quickly. Naval air reconnaissance early in the morning of May 13 indicated that the *Mayaguez* was still docked at Koh Tang; U.S. officials assumed that her crew was on the island, too. Late that night in Washington, Ford called together his national security team to go over the military options. The meeting was interrupted by the news that navy fighters had attacked a Cambodian flotilla heading to the mainland from Koh Tang Island. After sinking three of the boats, the squadron radioed that one pilot thought he saw "Caucasian faces" on another. Ford immediately ordered a halt to the attack — fortunately, since those indeed belonged to the thirty-nine *Mayaguez* crewmen.[6] The next afternoon, still unsure where the American merchant sailors were, Ford ordered a full-scale military rescue operation. Helicopters would lower some marines onto the *Mayaguez* and others onto Koh Tang as U.S. jets bombed mainland installations to keep the Cambodians from sending in reinforcements. The first helicopter to near Koh Tang was shot down in a portent of the blistering defense the Cambodians mounted. Yet, two minutes earlier, the

189

official Phnom Penh radio service had begun broadcasting allegations that the *Mayaguez* was a spy ship — followed by the announcement that they would release it. Whether the crew would also be released was not mentioned.

Although it was too late to abort the U.S. attacks already in progress, President Ford ordered that the Cambodians be informed that the military operation would be halted immediately upon the release of the thirty-nine American seamen. With no other means to deliver the message, Kissinger got press secretary Ron Nessen to put it out on the Associated Press international wire in hope that Cambodia's leaders would see it.[7] In the meantime, Ford decided to let the bombers begin their assault on the mainland.

As the marines tried to recapture the *Mayaguez* and battled unexpectedly strong Cambodian forces on Koh Tang Island, they discovered that the merchant crewmen were being held in the targeted port of Kompong Som. They were also being treated as cordially as ever. "The first man who spoke English greeted us with a handshake and welcomed us to Cambodia," recalled the ship's captain, Charles T. Miller. "He wanted to know if we were CIA or if we were FBI." Miller and his men managed to persuade their captor they were neither, and that their cargo ship had had nothing to do with American espionage or military operations. With that — and just a few hours after the U.S. military rescue assaults had begun — the crew was released. The Cambodians put them on a commandeered Thai fishing vessel, gave them white sheets to wave at their rescuers, and set them off back to the *Mayaguez* anchored at Koh Tang, which by then had turned into a war zone. Fortunately, the sheets did their trick, the fishing boat's intent was recognized, and the entire *Mayaguez* crew was safely transferred onto a U.S. destroyer.

Although the mission had been accomplished, the operation wasn't over. The marines who had landed on Koh Tang were still engaged in a brutal firefight with several hundred powerfully armed Cambodian troops they hadn't expected to find there — or to have the firepower to take out eight of the nine U.S. helicopters sent to the island.

The *Mayaguez* and her crew would be safely back at sea on their original course the next day, but at the high price of forty-one of their rescuers' lives. Later Captain Miller would lament, "I talked to the Marine major in the first chopper that was shot down, who had about a quarter of his back torn off by shrapnel. I cried. People were being killed to save me." Another seaman exclaimed, "After the Marines came, God I felt good. Damn good. Those Marines are great. Ford did a damn good job, but I just want to thank those Marines."

Many Americans, including some mainstream media figures, agreed that the president had done a damn good job. *Newsweek* called the *Mayaguez* rescue "a daring show of nerve and steel . . . swift and tough — and it worked." *New York Times* columnist Cyrus L. Sulzberger gushed that thanks to President Ford's "resolute and skillful leadership" in the crisis, "a polluting American image of lassitude, uncertainty and pessimism" had vanished. Republican senator Barry Goldwater summed up the feelings of the broader American public, remarking, "It was wonderful, it shows we've still got balls in this country."[8] Gerald Ford himself would boast in his memoir, "All of a sudden, the gloomy national mood began to fade. Many people's faith in their country was restored and my standing in the polls shot up 11 points."[9] Ford would have the *Mayaguez*'s bell placed on his Oval Office desk as a sign of American resolve.[10]

The general acclaim for the commander

in chief's swift and decisive handling of the *Mayaguez* incident was, naturally, offset by some harsh criticism that Ford had over-reacted, ordering a disproportionate military response just to prove his own toughness. Far more disturbing charges that the entire episode had been cooked up to bolster American public morale would prompt Ron Nessen to assert, "I never saw a shred of evidence that the *Mayaguez* was deliberately allowed to sail into a Cambodian trap in order to provoke an international inci-dent."[11] For his part, Henry Kissinger recalled replying to such allegations at a State Department press conference on May 16, 1975, "We were not looking for op-portunities to prove our manhood, only that it was essential for America's global role in the wake of the fall of Saigon to establish that there were limits beyond which the United States could not be pushed." Prais-ing President Ford for assessing the *Maya-guez* affair the same way in a May 23 interview for European television, Kissinger added, "What Ford had said was true, but it could not alter the reality that we had entered Indochina to save a country, and that we had ended by rescuing a ship."[12]

For all its success both as a rescue mis-sion and as public relations, the *Mayaguez* episode also revealed some serious problems in the White House. The troubles arose from the escalating infighting among Ford's senior advisers, more than a few of whose impressive egos seemingly put their self-interests above the nation's. In retrospect, the constant backbiting among his staff tarnished many of Ford's finer moments in 1975.

After nine months in office, the Ford administration's internal schisms no longer fell cleanly along the line between Nixon holdovers and Ford newcomers. As ambitious members of each camp gravitated toward their like-minded peers and superiors in the other, the cliques within the White House had quickly reconfigured, breaking between Kissinger people and those who were not, no matter whether they'd worked for Nixon. The most gaping breach grew between the secretaries of state and defense, as the *Mayaguez* incident showed.

Immediately after the cargo ship's capture, Secretary of State Kissinger had advocated mounting an all-out military assault against those who had commandeered it — perpetrators he broadly defined as the new Khmer Rouge government. Wanting to put the fear of the United States in them, Kissinger argued that B-52 bombing strikes on mainland targets would not only protect the rescue mission at hand but make it perfectly clear to the Cambodians and the rest of the world that the United States was not to be toyed with.

Secretary of Defense James Schlesinger, normally hawkish, adamantly opposed B-52 strikes on the mainland, with all their evil echoes of Nixon's — and Kissinger's — brutal 1973 B-52 bombings of Cambodia. Schlesinger argued that overreacting to the seizure of the *Mayaguez* could be disastrous, and was completely unnecessary in any case. It was possible, he pointed out, that what could be taken as an aggressive act might just be a mistake, and an easily fixed one at that. As it turned out, Schlesinger proved right, and even the actual tactical bombing of the mainland was not only overkill but also contributed absolutely nothing to the resolution of the affair. That, however, was not the point. President Ford, as commander in chief, had ultimately ordered four bombing waves, and Schlesinger had personally reported to him when the first had been "completed." That report began what Ford called in his memoir "some high-level bumbling at the Defense Department." In fact, the first wave had performed "armed reconnaissance," according to the Pentagon, and dropped no bombs. "The first strike never tool place, although we were told it had been 'completed,'" Ford would write.

After allowing that communications or technical problems may have caused confusion that hampered the first wave, Ford continued: "What is harder for me to understand is why the fourth air strike — and I had specifically ordered four — was never carried out. I hadn't told anyone to cancel that attack. Apparently, someone had, and I was anxious to find out who had contravened my authority. The explanations I received from the Pentagon were not satisfactory at all, and direct answers kept eluding me. Perhaps I should have pursued my inquiry, but since we had achieved our objective, I let the matter drop."[13]

Encouraged by high approval polls, on July 8, 1975, President Ford announced his candidacy for the 1976 Republican presidential nomination. After promising to run a clean campaign, Ford declared: "I will not forget my initial pledge to be President of all of the people. I believe I can best represent my party, but this will be futile unless I unite the majority of Americans who acknowledge no absolute party loyalty. Therefore, I will seek the support of all who believe in the fundamental values of duty, decency, and constructive debate on the great issues we face together as free people."[14]

Along those lines, three weeks later Ford attended the Conference on Security and Cooperation in Europe (CSCE) in Helsinki. Ford's participation proved controversial from the start. And it would haunt him ever after, losing him much crucial support among conservative Republicans. Yet, with their calls for openness and respect for human rights, the Helsinki Accords would mark the beginning of the end of the Soviet domination of Eastern Europe. Ford's attendance at the Soviet-sponsored conference substantially boosted the credibility of the ensuing Helsinki Accords, which became one of the finer legacies of his presidency. The agreement reflected everything that was best about Jerry Ford: long-term thinking, his deep-seated internationalism, and his belief in engagement rather than aggression, in matters large and small.

The CSCE, which opened in the Finnish capital on July 30, marked the largest assembly of European heads of state or government since the Congress of Vienna in 1815. For nearly three years, diplomats from each of the thirty-five countries had been niggling over a treaty scheduled to be signed at the conference. The document that emerged from these prolonged negotiations appeared as tepid and universally unobjectionable as one might expect. The proposed treaty airily covered three broad areas of concern: respecting the sovereignty of nations and the inviolability of their borders; lowering barriers to economic, scientific, and cultural cooperation and exchanges; and recognizing human rights. The Helsinki Final Act made no mention of any particular situations to which its vague provisions might apply, nor did it spell out any consequences for noncompliance. Basically, it provided a guideline for future civilized conduct in Europe. Yet as toothless as the Helsinki Accords seemed, no previous agreement had ever offered any guarantee of human rights of citizens in Eastern bloc nations — including the Soviet Union.

Before the CSCE summit, the United States had never made much of the human rights issue. As the scholar William Korey put it, the Nixon White House, "guided by national security advisor Henry A. Kissinger, looked upon the rights issue as unwarrantedly threatening to the Soviet Union at a time when Washington was pursuing its own bilateral détente with Moscow."[15] That attitude would change under the presidency of Gerald Ford, who believed that emphasizing human rights fell entirely in line with the ultimate goals of détente.

And that explained why so many Americans vigorously opposed Ford's trip to Helsinki. America's hawks had never embraced Richard Nixon's forays at thawing the Cold War. They preferred that détente remain unsupported by any agreement outside the existing SALT I treaty, which dealt strictly with quantities of arms, not ideology. Hardliners on both sides fervently maintained that preserving the state of undeclared, unprosecuted war would allow their system to prevail eventually.

However, just as Ford was firming up his plans to travel to Helsinki, the dissident Soviet writer Aleksandr Solzhenitsyn was stirring up anti-Soviet feeling in the United States. Solzhenitsyn, whose terrifying novel *The Gulag Archipelago* had just been published in English, had been awarded the 1970 Nobel Prize for Literature for his works on the cruelties of the Soviet political system, none of which were then available in his native land. Dissident lines about the totalitarian Soviets' "unwiped jackboots of the unsleeping State Security operatives" grabbed the attention of the Kremlin.[16] Arrested by the KGB and charged with treason for his revelations, Solzhenitsyn was deported to West Germany in February 1974, and he immigrated to the United States early the following year. Instantly sought after across America, Solzhenitsyn quickly tired of the spotlight and sought refuge on a farm in Vermont, where he resumed writing against the Soviet totalitarian state. On June 30, however, at the behest of the anti-Communist U.S. labor leader George Meany, Solzhenitsyn made a speech at an AFL-CIO dinner in Washington, excoriating not only the Soviet system but also any attempt at accommodation with it.

Coming less than a month before the Helsinki conference, Solzhenitsyn's urgent call for U.S. action against Communist brutality was seized upon immediately by conservative Republican senators Jesse Helms of North Carolina and Strom Thurmond of South Carolina, who on July 2 jointly requested that President Ford meet with Solzhenitsyn before the dissident left the nation's capital three days later. Ford refused.[17] Unfortunately, the White House failed to firmly enough cite the reason as the outrage against protocol of making demands on the president's time with less than half a week's notice. Instead, as Ford himself would admit in his memoir, "I decided to subordinate political gains to foreign policy considerations."[18]

In truth, Ford's motives for going to Helsinki had less to do with promoting "security and cooperation" in Europe than with pushing SALT II, the prospective follow-on arms control agreement he craved. Certain that he had made headway toward such a treaty in Vladivostok eight months earlier, Ford believed that putting the final pieces of it together during talks with Leonid Brezhnev in Helsinki before the eyes of the world would go a long way toward ensuring the arms agreement's success. What's more, although he never quite admitted so, Ford also felt that, if he could swing it, SALT II would stand as the hallmark of his presidency. Achieving that goal largely depended on enhancing the fine rapport he had established with the Soviet leader in Vladivostok. Doing so would not be easy if he had met with Solzhenitsyn just before the Helsinki congress. So Ford had it conveyed to the interested senators that he would be happy to meet with the dissident after he returned from Finland. The offer was apparently lost on opponents of détente. To these Cold Warriors, the prospective CSCE agreement proposed an intolerable implied acceptance of Soviet domination of the entire Eastern bloc. Even simpler to rail against was the president's so-called snub of the Soviet Union's best-known critic. "Does President Ford know the difference between détente and appeasement?" wondered the *New York Times.* "This unlikely question arises in light of the news that President Ford decided not to receive Nobel Laureate Aleksandr I. Solzhenitsyn because to do so would be inconsistent with détente."[19]

Washington Post syndicated columnist Joseph Kraft offered a rare, if implicit, defense of the president. After hearing Solzhenitsyn's speech in Washington about his experience in Soviet work camps and his resulting thoughts on labor-management relations and international affairs, the veteran newspaperman seemed less than impressed. "Because Solzhenitsyn's views have so little to do with practical American reality," Kraft opined, "the worship of his presence seems to me slightly ominous. I detect more than well-earned homage to a great artist. I sense a nostalgia for the simple certitudes of the cold war, a hankering . . . for a time when responsible behavior consisted of taking a stand against communism."

Kraft continued, "I happen to believe that American leaders have frequently let down their guard in dealing with the Soviet Union. But the application of an intense personal morality to international relations does not yield good policies."[20] Of course, the columnist didn't know that in private, President Ford had called Solzhenitsyn "a goddamn horse's ass," according to press secretary Ron Nessen, who added that "Ford complained that the dissident Russian writer wanted to visit the White House primarily to publicize his books and drum up lecture dates."[21] (In a 2003 interview, Ford admitted that his assessment of Solzhenitsyn back then was too harsh. "Maybe I should have met him *after* Helsinki," Ford said. "I learned to realize that his dissent was heartfelt and courageous.")[22]

The contentions leading up to Ford's trip were exacerbated by the opposition, or at least ambivalence, to the Helsinki Congress of many members of his own administration. Henry Kissinger was overheard calling the Helsinki Accords a "bunch of crappy ideas."[23] Only Jerry Ford seemed genuinely enthusiastic about the talks, as he revealed in a speech just before he left for Europe. "I know there are some honest doubts and disagreements among good Americans about this meeting," the president acknowledged. "There are those who fear the conference will put a seal of approval on the political division of Europe that has existed since the Soviet Union incorporated the Baltic nations and set new boundaries elsewhere in Europe by military action in World War II. . . . On the other extreme there are critics who say the meeting is a meaningless exercise because the Helsinki declarations are merely statements of principles and good intentions which are neither legally binding nor enforceable."

Emphasizing that the CSCE's proposed agreement did not call upon the West to cede anything that had not already been formalized in previous treaties, Ford laid out the main reason for his participation. "We are getting a public commitment by the leaders of the more closed and controlled countries to a greater measure of freedom and movement for individuals, information and ideas than has existed there in the past and establishing a yardstick by which the world can measure how well they live up to the stated intentions," he said. "It is a step in the direction of a greater degree of European community, of expanding East-West contacts, of more normal and healthier relations in an area where we have the closest historic ties. Surely this is in the best interest of the United States and of peace in the world."[24]

To prove his commitment to the gathering's goals, Ford dutifully sat through all thirty-four of his counterparts' speeches over the three days of the conference. Whatever that show of stamina proved, to Ford's own mind the trip hardly counted as a success because his talks with Brezhnev on SALT II went nowhere. Moreover, the negative reaction to his effort back home — particularly from the GOP right — continued upon his return. "The conference seating was all by alphabet," Ford recalled. "You know where I sat? With Brezhnev on one side of me and Erich Honecker of East Germany on the other. . . . The Right lambasted me to pieces."[25] But the long-term results of the CSCE would prove him right to have participated. "Conservatives were upset," *Detroit News* columnist Thomas J. Bray wrote in a 2004 profile of Ford, "for the accords seemed to ratify Soviet domination of Eastern Europe in return for vague promises by Moscow to adhere to human rights conventions."[26]

"At the same time of the Helsinki Summit," career U.S. diplomat Sandy Vogelsang wrote in 1979, "much of the U.S. press and many American politicians, disturbed by the apparent blessing to postwar borders in Europe, saw that meeting as a symbol of the Ford Administration's sell-out to the Soviet Union. Since then, dissidents throughout the U.S.S.R. and Eastern Europe have seized [upon] the [Helsinki accord] as a means to press their human rights cases or seek escape to the West. The act has thus acquired a momentum of its own."[27] Or, as Ford's White House chief of protocol, Henry E. Catto Jr., summed up in his memoir *Ambassadors at Sea,* "The right wing in the United States howled that the agreement was a sellout, which was nonsense, for the Helsinki agreement proved a splendid club with which to whack the Soviets when they violated human rights."[28]

Indeed, as a result of the accord, a number of Helsinki Commissions on Human Rights sprang up across the Soviet Union, as well as in its satellites and in other European nations, and proved very effective at shepherding individual cases to justice. The U.S. commission, originally sponsored by Republican representative Millicent Fenwick of New Jersey, investigated not domestic but Soviet human rights violations, indicating the extent to which the Helsinki Accords should focus on Communist states and how to fix them. That certainly wasn't what the Soviets had in mind when they first suggested a European security conference in 1954. And the Politburo most definitely did not foresee how the Helsinki Commissions' work would contribute to the fall of communism in 1989 by offering protection to dissident leaders such as Poland's Lech Walesa and Czechoslovakia's Václav Havel.

Just before he left for the conference, President Ford noted, "I saw an editorial the other day entitled 'Jerry Don't Go.' " (It appeared in the *Wall Street Journal* on July 23, 1975.) "But I would rather read that," Ford continued, "than headlines all over Europe saying, 'United States Boycotts Peace Hopes.' "

The Helsinki Accords, signed by the United States, Canada, and most European nations on August 1, agreed to honor human rights, cooperate in humanitarian, scientific, and economic affairs, and adhere to post–World War II national boundaries in Europe. A new era of U.S.-Soviet cooperation appeared to be launched. Around the time of the Helsinki conference, a U.S. Apollo spacecraft and a Soviet Soyuz docked in orbit. The sight of astronauts and cosmonauts shaking hands in space was interpreted as *rapprochement extraordinaire.*

Less than a year later, on May 28, 1976, Ford and Brezhnev signed the Treaty on Underground Nuclear Explosions for Peaceful Purposes, limiting underground testing.

But cooperative space gambits and vodka toasts belied the reality. The Helsinki Accords were Ford's greatest presidential achievement on the world stage, and an argument can be made that it proved to be the beginning of the end of the Soviet empire. "We went to Helsinki, and boy did I catch hell," Ford recalled in 2003. "Well, that human rights provision was the catalyst that brought about the demise of the Soviet Union because it gave inspiration and justification to the dissidents in the Soviet Union. This provision justified the dissidents doing everything they could to throw the bastards out. We got it started, then Jimmy Carter carried it on. It was the key to the destruction, the elimination of the Soviet Union. Sometimes if you're right you come out all right in history."[29]

9
LOOKING FOR TRACTION

With the 1976 presidential election on the horizon, many in Washington thought little of Gerald Ford's chances for success. The Nixon pardon retained its corrosiveness, as many Americans believed that Ford had engineered yet another Nixon cover-up, that he was nothing more than a patsy for the ex-president they loathed as "Tricky Dick." Also swirling around Washington official-dom was the churlish notion that Ford was an impostor president, a glorified caretaker who never could have gotten elected in his own right. As White House press secretary Ron Nessen remembered, Chief of Staff Donald Rumsfeld remarked late in 1974, "At the end of three months, the Ford administration will either have the smell of life or the smell of death. . . . If it's the smell of death, this White House is going to be torn to pieces by the press, by the Democrats, even by other Republicans who will challenge the president for the nomination in 1976."[1]

The pardon, however, was just one of Ford's public relations problems. Virtually everything Gerald Ford accomplished during his abbreviated term in the White House helped to doom his chances of winning the presidency in his own right in 1976. Ironically, the opposition to his policy achievements came not from the Democrats but from his own Republican Party. Many GOP leaders deemed Ford's policies way too liberal. Sparked in part by his trip to Finland, the tensions roiling the conservative ranks in 1975 would change the GOP for good, and presented the president with a dilemma: if he did what it would take to win his party's presidential nomination, he wouldn't have a prayer to win the general election — but if he did what would make him competitive the next November, he could well lose the Republican nomination he needed to get that far.

In the wake of Watergate and the Nixon pardon, the Democrats tightened their hold on Congress. Ford, for his part, vetoed fifteen bills in his first three months in office, more than Nixon had in the eighteen months preceding his resignation. However, Ford had a higher percentage of those vetoes overridden than any other twentieth-century president. "You've got to consider how tough it was for me to operate from the center," Ford recalled. "Liberal Democrats controlled the Senate and Congress. They wanted me marginalized. The conservative Republicans were all about Goldwater-Reagan. . . . They disdained my pulling out of Vietnam, the Helsinki trip and draft amnesty promise. And the media, having forced Nixon to resign, was just overflowing with venom."[2]

The journalist Richard Reeves observed that as of mid-1975, Ford had had less success leading Congress than any new president in recent history. It seemed as if every major bill Ford supported was treated like a flaming cowpie. After taking over from Nixon, Ford won just 58 percent of the 122 congressional votes on which there was a clear White House position, a record that compared badly with the 80 to 90 percent win records scored by Presidents Eisenhower, Kennedy, Johnson, and Nixon in their first congressional confrontations — it was even worse than the 60 percent scored by Nixon on 136 votes during the traumatic last eight months of his presidency.[3] Conservative Republicans like William A. Rusher, the publisher of *National Review,* saw an insurmountable and emblematic problem in Ford's choice of vice president. "Nixon's 1972 victory had been the by-product of a newly forged and distinctly fragile coalition of economic and social conservatives," Rusher explained in his 1984 book *The Rise of the Right.* "Victory for the Republican Party, at least for the foreseeable future, involved nurturing that coalition and making it permanent. For that purpose, the designation of Nelson Rockefeller . . . as vice president was not only pointless but downright counterproductive. Rockefeller represented virtually everything that antagonized social conservatives."[4] As the historian Herbert S. Parmet put it, "His presence accelerated the rebellion from what Kevin Phillips called the 'new right.' "[5]

Ford had had no intention of antagonizing his own party's powerful right wing when he picked Rockefeller. To the contrary, Ford had meant the choice to signal his desire to bring the Republican Party together, under a tent big enough to accommodate every view from his own up-by-the-bootstraps heartland conservatism to the progressive stands on social issues espoused by the Rockefeller Republicans. Ford was so proud of the move, in fact, that when asked at a November 14, 1974, press conference what he had achieved in his first hundred days in office, he replied: "Number one, nominating Nelson Rockefeller."[6]

Rockefeller's performance as vice president was faultless. He hewed loyally to the president's positions, at all times treating Ford with a properly humble deference. Moreover, he completed his boss's assignments better than capably, avidly presiding over advisory panels on issues from national health insurance to intelligence reform, in the latter case issuing the well-regarded Rockefeller Commission report on domestic espionage and other alleged illegalities by the Central Intelligence Agency.

But this wasn't good enough for GOP's conservatives, who at the 1964 Republican National Convention had booed Rockefeller off the stage before they anointed Barry Goldwater. The faithful objected to what Nelson Rockefeller represented, not to what the real man was. Firing him would be a first step toward realigning the entire Republican Party to the right. The former New York governor made stabs at conciliating the right by pandering to ultraconservatives down South — going so far as to appear with arch-segregationist governor George C. Wallace of Alabama and reaching out to Barry Goldwater and other libertarians. But the party's hard-liners wouldn't bend.

With his right flank permanently at odds with him for putting the paradigm of the Eastern Republican establishment within a heartbeat of the presidency, Ford thus had good reason for concern about his electoral prospects in 1976. He well knew that his finest accomplishments as president — getting the United States out of Vietnam, offering amnesty to the draft resisters, and supporting the Helsinki Accords — had hurt his standing among the more conservative members of his party. What's more, he knew that this time even his good-guy image wouldn't be enough, co-opted as it increasingly was by the surging Democratic challenger, Jimmy Carter. The former Georgia governor used his born-again Christianity and peanut farmer populism to define himself as an even more decent human being than the Republican incumbent. "Carter was running on 'I'll never tell a lie,' " Ford recalled. "I had the albatross of having pardoned Nixon, a known liar."[7]

Everywhere Ford looked in 1975, trouble loomed. Kissinger's famed Middle East shuttle diplomacy — which had wrought the Egyptian-Israeli accord of 1974 — hit a sudden dead end. The new Israeli government of Yitzhak Rabin, according to Kissinger, went "shivering in fear" every time Jordan was even mentioned.[8] Then, in March 1975, Kissinger, hoping for "Sinai II," tried to convince Rabin to withdraw from the mountain passes of Gidi and Mitla, to pull back in the Sinai about fifteen miles; Rabin flat-out refused. Annoyed that the Israelis were being stubborn, Ford sent a blistering cable to Jerusalem on March 21. "I am disappointed," Ford wrote, "to learn that Israel has not moved as far as it might." If diplomatic negotiations broke down over Sinai II, Ford threatened that America would "reassess" its entire Middle East strategy, including "our policy toward Israel."[9]

These were tough words from Ford — very tough. "It was about as brutal as such diplomatic letters get," the historian Walter Isaacson later wrote, "and the Israeli cabinet was shell-shocked." But Rabin refused to be intimidated. Despite a gallant effort, Israel wasn't going to give up a kilometer of the Sinai desert. Returning to Washington with no deal, Kissinger, on the flight home, carped (off the record) that Rabin was "a small man," and that for the peace process to continue, Israel needed a brave leader like Golda Meir. With Ford's approval, the State Department and NSC both issued

Middle East "reassessment" memoranda.[10]

Eventually, persistence prevailed. On August 21, after twelve days of negotiations in Jerusalem, Kissinger secured a Sinai II agreement. What turned the Israeli government around was the Ford administration's pledge for approximately $2.6 billion in military aid (including F-16 fighter jets). As Richard Valerian of NBC News put it, Sinai II was "the best agreement money could buy."

But Vietnam and the Middle East weren't the only regions causing the Ford administration fits. The U.S.-sponsored government in Cambodia, headed by Lon Nol, had been toppled by the Khmer Rouge. Since February 1973, the United States had dropped more than 250,000 tons of bombs on Cambodia, hoping to disable the Khmer Rouge — it only strengthened the insurgency movement. NATO ally Portugal, after a failed coup attempt, was drifting ever closer to the Soviet Union. A civil war in Angola was destablizing Africa. Worse, the major rebel cadre was being bankrolled by the unacceptable combination of Cuban troops and Kremlin aid. Add to the mix the strenuous opposition to SALT II by Senator Jackson and others and the result was a dismal foreign policy. "Every time we tried to move the ball forward," Ford recalled, "we seemed to lose ground. Eventually we got Sinai II and Portugal stayed in NATO and SALT II stayed alive into the Carter years but we were in a hard yardage situation. Perhaps the good news was we were getting America out of wars, not into them."[11]

Meanwhile, the U.S. economy could not have been worse for Ford in his first full year in office. If the public associated his term in office with the nation's dreadful fiscal condition, it would be another large hurdle for his election campaign to handle. When Ford assumed the presidency in August 1974, the U.S. Gross National Product was plummeting by 4.2 percent a year, consumer prices were soaring an annual 16.8 percent, and home-mortgage interest rates remained mired above 10 percent. By the end of Ford's first month in office, the Dow Jones Industrial Average had fallen ninety-nine points (a very significant drop at the time), followed by another fifty-point drop the week after he pardoned Nixon, combining to account for the sharpest stock-market dive in one month since the fall of 1929.[12] In January 1975, the U.S. unemployment rate rose by a full 1 percent, meaning a million Americans found themselves newly out of work in the space of a single month. Four months later, the jobless rate hit a peak of 8.9 percent. It would not be until the end of 1975 that the economy would begin to turn around, led by the halving of the inflation rate from the daunting 12 percent Ford faced when he took office.[13]

The economic news only fueled conservatives' ire. To Ford's dismay, it looked ever more likely that the Far Right's chosen champion, Ronald Reagan, would challenge him for the GOP nomination. The White House staff swept chaotically into action to keep that from happening, but their efforts went nowhere. Ford opened his gambit to hang on to the Right's support by naming nails-tough, Georgia-bred Secretary of the Army Howard "Bo" Callaway to manage his campaign. Callaway immediately set to courting his fellow arch-conservatives by publicly disparaging Vice President Rockefeller and his fitness for the Republican ticket. Ford did nothing to stop his own campaign from humiliating the distinguished public servant he had so proudly chosen. "My not defending Nelson at this juncture is my biggest professional regret," Ford later said. "He was a good man. I should have gone to bat for him."[14]

The president's appeal to the right wing

was not helped by First Lady Betty Ford's appearance on the CBS News program *60 Minutes* in August 1975. Although most of the American public liked and admired Betty Ford for her lively independence — and thought well of her husband for calling her his most trusted adviser — many conservatives took violent exception to the First Lady's apparent unconcern that her children had "probably" tried marijuana, not to mention to her response that she "wouldn't be surprised" if her teenage daughter, as "a perfectly normal human being like all young girls," were to have a premarital "affair." Even worse, as the right-wingers were concerned, Betty Ford also told the interviewer, Morley Safer, that she considered *Roe v. Wade,* the 1973 Supreme Court ruling legalizing abortion, "the best thing in the world . . . a great, great decision."[15]

Summarizing the Right's ensuing outrage, the *National Review* joked that "Mrs. Ford ought to know that it is not up to her to rewrite the Ten Commandments on nationwide TV."[16] Her husband felt compelled to issue a quick statement to the effect that although he supported his wife's right to speak out, her opinions were entirely her own.

As he had demonstrated throughout his

career in Congress, Gerald Ford had as keen an eye for good, and bad, publicity as any politician in the country. During his first hundred days in office, he had vastly expanded the White House PR staff.[17] Ford beefed up his own contributions to the PR effort soon after announcing his bid for the 1976 Republican presidential nomination. He increasingly hit the road to make personal appearances across the nation. Although he tried hard to look more like a caring leader reaching out to his constituents than a hungry candidate flat-out campaigning for votes, Ford couldn't help but want to counter Ronald Reagan's undeclared stumping around the country. For starters, Reagan was telling Republican audiences in city after city that he, and not Ford, was the true ideological heir to the party's 1972 landslide. "The mandate registered by the people still remains," Reagan declared. "The people have not changed in philosophy."[18] Just by making that backhanded swipe at Ford's claim to lead the GOP, Reagan again succeeded at sapping some of the president's support within the party.

Within the United States there was still residual 1960s-style anarchism erupting in the streets, the status quo being attacked from all corners. On January 29, the Weather Underground bombed the U.S. State Department headquarters in Washington, while on June 27 two FBI agents were killed in a shootout at the Pine Ridge Indian Reservation in South Dakota. Teamsters Union president Jimmy Hoffa was reported missing (presumed kidnapped or killed). In late December a bomb exploded at New York's LaGuardia Airport, killing eleven. Some people called it a Year of Bad Karma. Ford wasn't immune from the violence: twice in 1975 he was almost assassinated, both times in California.

On September 5, the president was shaking hands in a crowd that had turned out to see him near the California state capitol in Sacramento when an odd-looking woman standing two feet away from Ford pulled out a gun and pointed it at him. Fortunately, the woman couldn't fire a shot before a Secret Service agent wrested the .45-caliber pistol from her hand, while the rest of the detail threw themselves on the president and hustled him into the capitol building. Minutes after the twenty-six-year-old perpetrator, Charles Manson follower Lynette "Squeaky" Fromme, had been arrested, handcuffed, and trundled off to jail, Ford calmly proceeded to his scheduled meeting with Governor Jerry Brown, who didn't even learn of the assassination attempt until forty minutes later, when Donald Rumsfeld interrupted the economic policy discussion to give the president the official report on the incident. After meeting with Brown, Ford made his speech to the California legislature — on crime — as planned.[19]

Soon after the news of Fromme's attack reached Congress, a proud GOP committeeman took the floor and proclaimed: "Mr. Chairman, I think the record should show that for the first time since McKinley, we have a Republican President worth shooting."[20] Apparently so, as practically the same thing happened again just seventeen days later.

The second attempt on Ford's life bore eerie similarities to the first. On September 22 the setting was again California, where the last event of the president's trip to San Francisco was a local television interview at the St. Francis Hotel. After the taping Ford walked out of the lobby and was heading to his limousine when a shot rang out. Rumsfeld and two Secret Service men pounced on the president and pushed him behind the car as bystanders seized gray-haired gunwoman Sara Jane Moore and her .38-caliber revolver. "The one shot Moore fired," Ron Nessen reported, "struck the wall of the hotel to Ford's right, ricocheted, struck the curb to Ford's left and, now spent, bounced up and hit a taxi driver in the groin."[21] As the police carted off Ford's second female would-be assassin that month, the president lay on the floor of his limo, uninjured despite being crushed under the considerable weight of two beefy Secret Service agents plus Donald Rumsfeld, all three of whom remained atop him as the motorcade sped away. "Can we turn on the air conditioning? It's getting stuffy in here," Ford cracked.[22]

Outwardly unfazed by the two attempts on his life, President Ford made it clear that the bizarre acts of two deranged women in California would have no effect on his public appearances. "Under no circumstances," he declared, "will I, and I hope others, capitulate to those that want to undercut what's good in America."[23] That said, although he did not reduce his travel appearances, at the Secret Service's insistence Ford began wearing bulletproof vests under his suit jackets when he went out in public. When asked in 2003 whether he had any nightmares after two assassination attempts, Ford claimed he told Betty, "I'm going to have to review my support for the

223

Equal Rights Amendment. These women are trying to kill me."[24]

Ronald Reagan, meanwhile, kept up his cross-country noncampaign. While Ford and his fretting staff waited for the former California governor to declare himself in or out of the presidential race, Reagan rolled merrily along, gathering momentum as he continued to pick up passionate support from bedrock conservatives, including a few with very deep pockets. A number of like-minded hard-core political pros also signed on to the Californian's righteous crusade. In truth, Ford and Reagan were both calling for pretty much the same platform the GOP had been pushing for decades: smaller government, less federal spending, and upward mobility by one's own bootstraps for all. But while their messages were essentially the same, the two men vying to be the Republicans' bicentennial-year messenger had little in common except their mutual antipathy.

"Several of his characteristics seemed to rule him out as a serious challenger," Ford recalled thinking of Reagan during those uncertain months of 1975. "One was his penchant for offering simplistic solutions to hideously complex problems. A second was his conviction that he was always right in every argument; he seemed unable to acknowledge that he might have made a mistake. Finally, I'd heard from people who knew him well that he liked to conserve his energy. From every campaign I'd witnessed, I knew that you can't run for President and expect to work only from nine to five."[25]

Reagan, who later proved that you can actually *be* president and work only nine to five, considered Nixon's successor weak. " 'Ford was not a leader,' Reagan told his intimates," reported his biographer Lou Cannon. "In private conversations, Reagan referred to him as a 'caretaker' who had been in Congress too long."[26] According to Cannon, Reagan also blamed Ford for the federal budget deficit, which had soared near $52 billion by that point. Willfully ignoring the president's obvious efforts to curb the deficit by repeatedly vetoing congressional spending bills, Reagan persisted in portraying the incumbent as entirely responsible for the government's outrageous debt. (Beginning just six years later, over his own two full terms in the White House, Ronald Reagan would send the nation's borrowing skyrocketing far higher, setting a new record of $1 trillion during his first year in office and breaking it each of the next two years.)

In reality, to fight the ongoing recession President Ford proposed a stimulative $28 billion tax cut in October 1975, an outgrowth of the plan to "cut taxes for most individual businesses," coupled with a request to Congress to cut an offsetting $28 billion in spending to keep the reduction in tax revenues from hiking the federal deficit and thereby spurring inflation even higher. Just before its winter recess, Congress approved the president's proposed tax cut but not the lower spending, leading Ford to veto the bill. Congress then responded by editing into the bill a vague pledge to try to rein in federal expenditures some other time. The president reluctantly signed the barely revised new version, in the hope that it would prove better for the economy than doing nothing.

Ford took his toughest stand against government spending in response to New York City's fiscal crisis. The nation's largest metropolis had long been its most profligate as well, shelling out twice as much as any other city in the country for services and salaries.[27] Since 1965, New York City's budget had tripled as its expenses had shot up by some 12 percent a year while its revenues grew only about 5 percent annually.[28] After a decade of recklessly unaffordable spending on ever more programs, employees, and raises, the Big Apple had put itself in a pickle. By April 1975, just to meet its bloated municipal payroll the city had racked up a whopping $14 billion in debt — most of it on wildly unfavorable terms. Worse, the loans were secured on pie-in-the-sky projections of highly unlikely future revenues, which city officials continued to put up as collateral for even more new loans.

That spring, the pyramid was starting to collapse as New York ran out of both cash and credit. "The city's politicians, Democrats and Republicans alike, had behaved so irresponsibly for so many years that a fiscal Armageddon was almost inevitable," Ford would recall in his memoir.[29] The finance capital of the world was teetering on the verge of bankruptcy.

Throughout the year, New York City mayor Abraham Beame and New York governor Hugh Carey went hat in hand to the White House to ask President Ford for a federal bailout in the form of ninety-day guarantees for $1 billion in new city bonds. Ford and his top economic advisers responded to the appeal by essentially telling the New Yorkers that it was their own fault their city was in this fix, as the Big Apple's own officials were the ones who had spent money like drunken sailors on a decade's shore leave. Stung by the administration's rude rejection, Carey declared it the product of a "level of arrogance and disregard for New York that rivals the worst days of Richard Nixon and his gang of cutthroats."[30]

Treasury Secretary William Simon, a Nixon holdover and former Wall Street investment banker, likewise excoriated the city's managers, labor unions, and even its commercial lenders for letting New York dig itself into such a deep pit. In Simon's view, the city could and should take the harsh steps needed to solve its own problems; throwing more money at them would only perpetuate the foolishness. President Ford and Federal Reserve Board Chairman Arthur F. Burns concurred, joining in advising their guests to implement sounder budget policies and cut less necessary municipal services. The message was clear: make the hard choices and you'll pull through somehow.

With no help forthcoming from Washington, at several points before the year was out New York indeed toed the brink of insolvency. But it managed to yank itself back every time by making just the kinds of drastic cuts the Ford administration had suggested, including the layoffs of forty thousand police, firefighters, sanitation workers, and other city employees. Many Americans outside the nation's biggest city applauded their president's tightfisted approach. "The country has long seen New York as arrogant," remarked one observant bond broker. "The attitude is, 'So now you're in trouble, then help yourself, Big Mouth!' "[31]

As New York City's financial woes worsened, Vice President Rockefeller advised Ford that his home state might be able to step in to help before the federal government had no choice but to do so. With Ford's approval, Rockefeller met with state Republican leaders that October. The vice president listened as the upstate pols laid out their concerns regarding the fiscal crisis. The New Yorkers understood, of course, that the administration's skinflint stance grew from Ford's need to court the conservative wing of his party away from the allure of Ronald Reagan — and that the Republican Right sneered at the very idea of a federal rescue for New York, of all places, from its own wretched excesses. That said, however, the state GOP's representatives also warned Rockefeller that unless the White House started treating New York City a little more nicely, Gerald Ford might as well forget about the state's mighty electoral vote come next November.

Rockefeller dutifully reported what he had heard back to the president. Ford listened to the New Yorkers' concerns. Their veiled threats, however, only stiffened his resistance to their entreaties for federal assistance until he saw proof of real belt-tightening in New York City. Ford's stance remained as firm as it had since his May meeting with Beame and Carey, who had come begging then without so much as a pie chart to show what New York intended to do with the federal aid they were asking for. "Beame and Carey had no answers. Nor did they have a plan," Ford recalled in his memoir. "And their demands were ridiculous. Apparently, they thought they could come down to Washington, employ scare tactics and roll over us. If the city went bankrupt, they warned, the effect on the banking community in the United States would be catastrophic."[32]

Ford still wasn't buying it five months later, although he did give Rockefeller permission to speak out on the crisis in New York on the grounds that it couldn't hurt, and might even help both the city and the vice president, at least politically. On October 12 Rockefeller made a speech in Manhattan that appeared to extend the metropolis a hint of sympathy, even while deflecting the blame for the lack of federal action off of the White House and onto Congress. The vice president's remarks went over fairly well with his audience, but they raised conservatives' hackles elsewhere and kicked up a firestorm in the West Wing. "There is no more continuous thread in the history of our Republic than White House wrath when Vice Presidents speak out of turn in public," explained Robert Hartmann, one of Rockefeller's few fans in Ford's inner circle. "Now they [Ford's other top advisers] said Rocky was really off the reservation, sabotaging the President's careful and nearly successful strategy, feathering his own New York nest, furthering his family's banking interests, fueling conservative rebellion in the South, West, and mid-America. Simon and Rumsfeld temporarily buried their old blood feud. The President was inundated with polls and polemics with a single theme: Rockefeller's gotta go."[33]

It was all over for Jerry Ford's right-hand man. First, at a press conference in Washington, the president firmly restated his — and thus his administration's — official lack of sympathy for the spendthrifts of New York, declaring: "I do not think it is a healthy

231

thing for the federal government to bail out a city, and I mean any city that has handled its fiscal affairs as irresponsibly over a long period of time as New York City has."[34] Then, on October 28, Ford dropped the boom on his vice president at their regular weekly meeting in the Oval Office. As ever, the tone between them stayed civil, even cordial, as the two old pros discussed the problematic political situation indicated by recent polls, which showed how gravely Rockefeller's presence on the ticket weakened the GOP's chances of keeping the White House. Finally, Ford wrote in his memoir, he told his vice president that, "to be brutally frank, some of these difficulties might be eliminated if you were to indicate that you didn't want to be on the ticket in 1976. I'm not *asking* you to do that, I'm just stating the facts."[35]

Rockefeller's unswerving loyalty to his commander in chief prompted him to offer to bow out immediately. Both men could then maintain that it had been the vice president's decision to withdraw from the 1976 ticket. But the fact remained that he had been pushed, and that Jerry Ford had chosen to do the pushing. Indeed, as Ron Nessen recalled, at the end of the huddle the president told Rockefeller, "Nelson, you're a hell of a team player."[36] Ford would later express misgivings about the move that he never mentioned at the time. "I was grateful for his expression of unselfishness," Ford confessed, "his willingness to do what was in the best interests of the party and the country — and me. At the same time, I was angry with myself for showing cowardice in not saying to the ultraconservatives, 'It's going to be Ford and Rockefeller, whatever the consequences.' "[37]

Ford's public change of mind about such a crucial decision as his choice of vice president — especially against his own inclinations, and less than a year after having called it his proudest achievement — not only made him look weak, it smacked of the most craven politicking. Whatever one may have thought of Rockefeller, it was difficult not to be disheartened by the way the president threw him over, so openly kowtowing to the noisiest rabble in his party. What's more, getting rid of Rockefeller didn't succeed in pushing Ronald Reagan out of the race.

"I am not appeased," Ford's rival replied when asked his opinion on Rockefeller's removal after the news was officially announced in early November.

If Ford hadn't already been about to lose New York state's hefty chunk of electoral votes for kicking its favorite son off his ticket, he certainly ended his chances when he further hardened his line against federal aid for its beleaguered city. In an October 29 speech at Washington's National Press Club, the president swore to veto any bill Congress might pass to bail New York City out of the morass caused by its own "fiscal mismanagement," on the grounds that to do so would allow its leaders to "escape responsibility for their past follies."[38] Noting that New York's "officials have proved in the past that they will not face up to the city's massive network of pressure groups as long as any other alternative is available," Ford cautioned: "If they can scare the whole country into providing that alternative now, why shouldn't they be confident they can scare us again three years from now?"[39] The next day, the front page of New York's *Daily News* blared the seventy-two-point bold headline "Ford to City: Drop Dead."[40]

The president was stung by the ensuing charges that he lacked compassion for all the little people in the big city who would be hurt by his ogrelike heartlessness. But Ford — whose core belief in the virtue of thrift had been instilled in him in boyhood by his revered parents' hardworking example — honestly thought that his "Dutch uncle approach" to New York's problems would not only work in the short term but give the city just the tough-love impetus it needed to put its finances in order for good. As he would explain to reporters later that year, "I think the decisions that I have made [that] have been hard, that on the surface appear at this time to be lacking in compassion, those decisions, in the long run, are going to be recognized as right. So it is a question of understanding at the moment that you have to take the long view, not the short view, in order to really indicate your compassion. And that is what I have tried to do."[41]

In the end, he succeeded in getting New York City to adopt more sensible financial practices. He provided the bailout its local officials had been begging for all along, on the condition that the city thereafter operate within austerity budgets imposed by Washington. The deal was accepted on November 26. Ford immediately asked Congress to pass legislation giving New York City access to up to $2.3 billion in direct federal loans in each of the next three years.[42] The lawmakers complied, and Ford signed the bill on December 9. When asked about the deal at a campaign session with local officials in Louisiana the next spring, Ford explained: "Because I was very firm in dealing with the Mayor and the Governor of New York, we finally worked out a program that I think, if they carry it out — and they are going to carry it out, or else — we can get them by their own bootstraps to straighten out their problem.

"We did agree," he went on, "to give them some money on a cash-flow basis because they have peaks where they get money and they have valleys where they have to spend it and their revenues don't equal their expenditures. But I can tell you that New York City is on schedule as far as we are concerned." The president added that a few weeks earlier the city had made its "first payback," of $270 million plus $5 million in interest. "So," he pointed out, "Uncle Sam didn't do too badly."[43]

Gerald Ford, on the other hand, wasn't doing too well with the American people. The heartland's schadenfreude toward New York didn't stand up against the thought of all those laid-off cops and firefighters. That fall, between his cold dismissal of Nelson Rockefeller and his harsh treatment of the Big Apple, good ol' Jerry Ford had begun to look awfully mean, not to mention disloyal, cynical, and somehow waffling and stubborn at the same time.

On November 28, however, Ford scored a touchdown by nominating Judge John Paul Stevens of the Seventh Circuit Court of Appeals in Chicago to replace William O. Douglas on the U.S. Supreme Court. Ford had been trying to get Douglas off the court since the mid-1960s and now the liberal justice had finally retired. All presidents covet the power to appoint a Supreme Court justice to cement their legacy. With the stakes high, usually a rough-and-tumble confirmation process ensues. That was not the case with Stevens. The U.S. Senate approved him by a 98 to 0 vote.

With the Stevens appointment, Ford was starting to define himself. He knew shake-ups were necessary if he wanted to de-Nixonize his White House. In addition to the official withdrawal of Nelson Rockefeller as his 1976 running mate, Ford announced on November 3 that James Schlesinger would be removed as secretary of defense in favor of the more trustworthy Donald Rumsfeld, who would in turn be replaced as White House chief of staff by his less excitable deputy, Dick Cheney. William E. Colby was out as CIA director, and George H. W. Bush was coming back from Beijing to take his place. Ambassador Elliot Richardson would likewise be called home from the Court of St. James's to take over as secretary of commerce from the ailing Rogers C. B. Morton, who would henceforth devote his efforts to Ford's campaign. Finally, in the move that generated by far the loudest buzz, Secretary of State Henry Kissinger would no longer serve concurrently as national security adviser. His deputy, air force lieutenant general Brent Scowcroft, would take over that role. The media dubbed the changes "The Halloween Massacre."[44]

The impetus of the Halloween Massacre, according to Ford, was his inability to tolerate the crude, daily backbiting between Kissinger and Schlesinger. "I was sick and tired of their irreconcilable views and personalities," Ford recalled. "Therefore, I had to make a choice. I chose Kissinger. I decided to call Schlesinger in on a Sunday morning. And I said, 'Jim, things aren't working out well on the cabinet level. I want to make a change and I'd like you to step aside and I'll appoint you as an ambassador someplace in Europe.' He said, 'I won't take that. Are you firing me?' And I said, 'If you put it that way, yes.' So he got up and walked off. So I put Rumsfeld in at

Defense."[45]

Displaying a share-the-pain approach, Ford next informed Kissinger that his portfolio was going to be reduced in half. "I went to Henry and I said, 'Henry, I'm going to take your NSC hat away from you because I think it's poor organization,' " Ford later explained. "Henry didn't like that too well. He said, 'The press will misinterpret that I am being demoted.' Well, you know Henry's famous ego. He was bruised. But I did it and I elevated Brent Scowcroft, his deputy, to head NSC. So that was a busy Sunday. It gave me a chance to put my imprimatur on my cabinet at a very important time."[46]

Although the president emphasized that his main motive for making these drastic personnel changes was to formalize the establishment of his "own team," whispers quickly arose that Rumsfeld had orchestrated the entire shake-up, mostly to get himself the Pentagon's top job, but also to get Kissinger out of the West Wing and Bush out of the running to replace Rockefeller as Ford's running mate.[47] Eager to deny any such thing, Rumsfeld pointedly informed the president that he would need a few days to think over Ford's offer. When a reporter for *Time* magazine asked Kissinger if he believed Rumsfeld really had any such reservations about taking the Pentagon's plum job, the secretary of state deadpanned, "Yes . . . and Nixon didn't want to be President."[48]

Whatever inspired the overhaul of the Ford administration, the results proved the moves a good idea. The White House operated far more smoothly under the low-key Cheney than it had when the contentious Rumsfeld was running the place, although the new staff coordinator exercised at least as much control, and before long wielded even more power than his predecessor. "Some reporters privately started calling him the Grand Teuton," Nessen remembered, a pun linking the mountains in Cheney's home state of Wyoming with the Prussian sensibility of H. R. Haldeman, who had ruled the White House with an iron fist for Nixon.[49]

Regardless of personnel shake-ups, the low ebb of U.S. foreign policy during Ford's White House tenure occurred on December 7, 1975. President Ford, along with Kissinger, was wrapping up a tour of Asia. Diplomacy in the region was getting more and more complicated; India, for example, just the previous year had detonated its first atomic bomb. After spending a few days in

China and then the Philippines, they headed to Indonesia, where Ford met with the country's thuggish dictator, General Haji Mohammad Suharto. At the time, East Timor, located in the Indonesian archipelago, was in the midst of an independence movement. A group called the Front for the Liberation of East Timor (FRETILIN) had taken to the streets demanding sovereignty. Portugal, the colonial power that had controlled East Timor for more than 450 years, pulled out. Suharto, however, wasn't going to allow independence to happen. Insisting that East Timor was part of Indonesia, he called up his troops with orders to invade East Timor and squash FRETILIN by whatever military means necessary.[50]

Ford and Kissinger approved Suharto's plans to invade East Timor. "You've got to remember that we just lost Vietnam," Ford recalled in a 2003 interview. "We didn't know whether the domino theory would occur throughout the region. Our main goal wasn't to alienate Indonesia from us. So when Suharto raised the imminent invasion of [East] Timor we didn't object. It was, I recall, only briefly discussed. To be honest, I had prepared mainly for my China meetings. The State Department was overseeing the Indonesia situation. I wasn't informed

241

properly, I guess."[51]

Documentary evidence proved that Ford-Kissinger acquiescence helped contribute to the genocide of approximately two hundred thousand East Timorians due to violence and famine. Armed with U.S.-made weapons, General Suharto's troops massacred about one-sixth of the nation's population. The butchering began only sixteen hours after Air Force One left Indonesian airspace. "Suharto was given the green light to do what he did," former CIA operations officer C. Philip Liechty recalled. "There was discussion in the Embassy and in traffic with the State Department about the problems that would be created for us if the public and Congress became aware of the level and type of military assistance that was given to Indonesia at that time. Without continued heavy U.S. military support the Indonesians might not have been able to pull it off."[52]

Obviously President Ford didn't want two hundred thousand East Timorese slaughtered. That year, in fact, the new independent nation-states of Angola, Cape Verde, Mozambique, Papua New Guinea, Suriname, and the Comoros became a geopolitical reality. And, to his credit, he never tried to cover up his meeting with Suharto.

"Look," Ford later recalled. "I don't want to pass the blame. Given the brutality that Indonesia exhibited in East Timor, our support was wrong. Henry was not infallible. I didn't realize just how bad the situation would become. You've got to understand that, in the scope of things, Indonesia wasn't too much on my radar. Hindsight is easy. I should have questioned Henry more about the situation. My record shows, like Helsinki, that I personally cared about human rights. I listened to the experts on Indonesia. That was a mistake. At the time, though, it didn't seem like a mistake. We needed allies after Vietnam. Henry — and I'm not exonerating myself — goofed."

When asked if he wanted to apologize to history for East Timor, Ford said, "Yes. I mean I truly, honestly feel for those families which suffered losses. I'm sorry for them. The whole thing was tragic but I only learned the extent to what happened there after I left Washington. Then it was too late."[53] The people of East Timor would have to wait until 2002 to gain their country's independence.

10
THE BICENTENNIAL
CAMPAIGN

Gerald Ford had reason for thanksgiving in November 1975. Although the Nixon pardon was a huge strike against him, a Gallup poll of registered Republicans showed him leading Ronald Reagan 58 to 36 percent, while a survey of the general electorate put him ahead of likely Democratic nominees by 50 to 42 percent.[1] Even Democratic National Committee chairman Robert S. Strauss had been forced to allow of Ford the previous June that, "You're not going to beat him with a more honest, honorable man. . . . You're going to beat him on the issues."[2] Strauss said that, of course, more than a year before the aggressively pious Jimmy Carter became the Democratic standard-bearer. Other elements also came into the foreground on the eve of the nation's bicentennial. As Kevin Phillips had predicted in his 1969 book *The Emerging Republican Majority,* "a populist revolt of the

American masses who have been elevated by prosperity to middle-class status and conservatism" was afoot "against the caste, policies and taxation of the mandarins of Establishment liberalism."[3] Eager to take advantage of this burgeoning trend, Ronald Reagan announced his candidacy for the Republican presidential nomination on November 20, 1975.

The former California governor proved adept at recasting Ford's strengths as weaknesses, and exploiting those. Having faced real-life situations requiring actual executive decisions, Ford had deviated from his party's narrow line as situations required, as every president must if he wants to get anything done, especially with Congress firmly in the hands of his opposition. But Reagan and his supporters pounced on every example of Ford's supposed apostasy. They squealed that Ford was betraying the conservative cause, all with a stridency forbidden the incumbent by the demands of comportment befitting a head of state. And no politician topped Reagan at smashing complex topics into tidy anecdotal aphorisms as irrefutable as they were specious. Or, in the words of James A. Baker III, Ford's campaign manager in 1976 and later Reagan's chief of staff and Treasury secretary, "Nobody ever accused the Gipper of being squishy on the issues."[4]

No one could rightly accuse Gerald Ford of it, either, though that didn't stop Ronald Reagan, whose swipes truly disconcerted Ford. The president always presented his views deliberately and defensibly, point by point. Reagan, by contrast, was running on oratorical extravagance. That contrast wouldn't change as the GOP primaries drew near. Ford campaigned as he always had, as a plainspoken man of the people, assuming it would play better than Reagan's hard-nosed, in-your-face charm. One of Ford's worst attributes as a candidate, however, was his inability to communicate over television. He spoke in a halting, adenoidal fashion, hesitating before making a policy point, often emphasizing the wrong word. His body language was off-kilter, as if he were a robot programmed to point his finger or shake his head "no." The net effect was a string of uninspiring, milquetoast televised stump speeches. "The president had a habit of pausing for several beats before he spoke," Baker recalled. "When the red light on a television camera would come on — his cue to talk — he would not start speaking right away. This sometimes gave the mistaken impression that he was

246

struggling to find the right words."[5]

A year before the 1976 election, Ford's campaign pollster, Robert Teeter, reported troubling findings regarding the president's public image. His surveys showed that too many of the American people harbored doubts about both the president's intelligence and his strength as a leader. This prompted Teeter to suggest that Ford "needs to appear more Presidential . . . to improve his perception as being knowledgeable and competent." His recommendation set the White House staff scurrying to come up with a spate of high-toned speeches and activities intended to make Ford look statesmanlike through the rest of his term. Most media coverage of the resulting events stressed their intent to paint the incumbent as "presidential."[6]

That December, *Newsweek* ran a cover story headlined "Ford in Trouble." Citing Reagan's surging popularity alongside Ford's failures to sway Congress his way, the article foresaw grim prospects for the man some dubbed "Bozo the President."[7] In the end, that jokey take on Gerald Ford would take on a life of its own, and would form the lasting image that hurt him more than anything else.

Quips at the expense of Ford's intellect

went back as far as Lyndon Johnson, who was credited with two of the best known: that "Jerry Ford is a nice guy, but he played too much football with his helmet off,"[8] and that Ford "is so dumb he can't fart and chew gum at the same time."[9] As the 1976 presidential campaign got going the gibes turned more topical, as *Time* noted in January, citing current jokes such as, "The president was loath to help New York during its fiscal crisis because he has bad memories of the city's great blackout; he was trapped for six hours on an escalator."[10] Of course, Ford didn't help matters by introducing California's GOP Senate candidate S. I. Hayakawa as "Dr. Haya-kama," prompting an aide to confess, "It was better than what he called Hayakawa in a private meeting. He called him 'Hiawatha' the first time."[11]

At least as hard to take as the charge of dumbness was the media's depiction of Ford as a clumsy oaf. For some reason, the sort of embarrassing everyday missteps the press had ignored in covering previous presidents became news when committed by Gerald Ford, be it stumbling on a Colorado ski slope, tripping on a church stairway, or bumping his head on the door to Air Force One. The media characterized him as a klutz. The comedian Chevy Chase's running slapstick routine as a bumbling Ford on *Saturday Night Live* became so well known that the president tried to defuse its impact by taping self-deprecating bits for an episode of the popular NBC comedy series. That particular ninety minutes was guest-hosted by his good-humored press secretary Ron Nessen in April 1976.[12] "Chevy definitely cost some votes," Ford later joked. "But I had to admit he was damn funny."[13] James Baker observed, "No one who knew the president ever quite understood Chevy Chase's *Saturday Night Live* impersonation of him as a genial dolt who stumbled over doorsteps and big words. Unfortunately, the caricature — particularly the physical humor — took on a life of its own."[14]

A decade after he left office, Ford wrote a book titled *Humor and the Presidency,* on the front flap of which he declared that as the "victim" of so much of it, "I take a backseat to no one as far as humor is concerned."[15] In his good-natured look at the comedy to be found in the White House, Ford explained how he "persevered in the face of humorous, satirical, or, on occasion, ridiculing assaults" a bit more seriously, writing: "Some people have suggested that I handled the jokes at my expense very well, and that I thought such things 'came with the turf' of being president. Let me put it this way: I developed a good exterior posture. The truth of the matter is that some of my favorite pipes have teeth marks in their stems that you wouldn't believe. This is a fact. You cannot cry out dramatically about your outrage or your indignity. That, as sure as tomorrow's sunrise, will open a floodgate that you'll never be able to close."[16]

In the spring of 1976, with his nation at peace and its economy picking up, the incumbent should have gained momentum. Instead, Ford's bid weakened heading into the primaries as he spent too much time responding to Reagan's endless barbs on relatively minor issues. Regarding the future of the Panama Canal, for example, Reagan got away with crowd-rousing conservative bromides such as "We built it, we paid for it, it's ours and we are going to keep it,"[17] leaving the president to detail the dull nuances behind the official U.S. position in the complex negotiations over the inevitable eventual transfer of control of the canal to Panama.

Despite the Reaganites' passionate efforts, Ford managed to hang on to enough of his party's faithful to win the first three big Republican primaries, in New Hampshire,

Florida, and Reagan's native state of Illinois. The last victory came despite press allegations on March 12 — four days before the Illinois contest — that Ford's campaign chairman, Bo Callaway, had misused his office as secretary of the army to secure a sweetheart Colorado land deal from the federal government. While answering the never-proven charges distracted Callaway — who was swiftly informed by Dick Cheney that he had to go, and did — and the rest of Ford's top campaign staff, Reagan stepped up his attacks and advertising and pulled off an upset in the North Carolina primary on March 23. The implications were huge. "Without his performance in North Carolina," Lou Cannon would explain, "Reagan would have faded from contention . . . and it is unlikely that he would have won the presidential nomination four years later."[18]

After taking his first primary, Reagan was not only back in the race but began to notch a string of victories earning him loads of delegates. Ford now focused on winning the hearts and minds of every uncommitted delegate. Republican delegates were brought to Washington for briefings and to meet the president. Some were even invited to the social high-point of the bicentennial year:

the state dinner for Queen Elizabeth II, who came to the capital in July to recognize two hundred years of independence for the former British colony.[19]

That summer, Ford used the bicentennial of America to bolster his campaign. Everywhere that Independence Day, buildings displayed patriotic bunting. Companies manufactured bicentennial-stamped products while Disneyland launched its Main Street Electrical Parade. CBS television ran regular "bicentennial minutes." A Freedom Train criss-crossed the nation displaying such national heirlooms as Dorothy's ruby slippers from *The Wizard of Oz* and a lunar rover from an Apollo moon mission. A large July Fourth cake was cut in Washington, D.C., while New York City hosted the Parade of Tall Ships on the Hudson River. President Ford spoke at numerous patriotic events, but it was his speech at Independence Hall in Philadelphia, written by Bob Hartmann, that truly captured the celebratory mood of the country. "From this small but beautiful building," Ford intoned, "then the most imposing structure in the Colonies, came the two great documents that continue to supply the moral and intellectual power for the American adventure in self-government."[20] Hartmann believed that the speech was "Ford at his very, very best."[21]

Overseeing the bicentennial celebration had given Ford presidential gravitas leading into the Republican National Convention that August in Kansas City. To seal the support of uncommitted delegates, however, Ford capitulated to Reagan's demand that the GOP platform include his proposed plank calling for "morality" in U.S. foreign policy making. Ron Nessen later recalled Dick Cheney countering Brent Scowcroft's objections to what amounted to an anti-Kissinger plank by explaining to the national security adviser, "Principle is okay up to a certain point . . . but principle doesn't do any good if you lose the nomination." Besides, Cheney added, "platforms don't mean anything; they are forgotten the day after the convention."[22]

In his speech accepting the nomination, Ford proclaimed: "I speak not of a Republican victory, but a victory for the American people. You at home listening tonight, you are the people who pay the taxes and obey the laws. You are the people who make our system work. You are the people who make America what it is. It is from your ranks that I come and on your side that I stand. . . . So, tonight, it is not the power and the glamor of the Presidency that leads me to ask for another four years. It is something every hardworking American will understand — the challenge of a job well begun, but far from finished. . . . My record is one of progress, not platitudes . . . of specifics, not smiles . . . of performance, not promises."[23]

Once Reagan's challenge ended, most of the right wing returned to Ford's side. As the conservative columnist James J. Kilpatrick wrote in *National Review,* "The appeal of the Old Reliable is likely to gain. The Ford record, in the conservative view, is not that bad. Yes, he has named a batch of moderate liberals to his Administration; yes, he has turned around on a dozen issues. But . . . the country, for the most part, is muddling contentedly along. If the threat of one-party rule under [Democratic nominee Jimmy] Carter is to be dispelled, it can be dispelled only by uniting behind Ford. Most conservative disgrunts, once they weary of futile bellyaching, will see it that way."[24]

And so Ford hung on to the conservatives' support, even if he didn't inspire their ardor. With just two and a half months to go before Election Day, all he had to do now was secure enough moderates and liberals to hold off Jimmy Carter.

Ford's ideological tug-of-war with Reagan in the primaries made that task all the harder. After he won the nomination, the incumbent was still reeling on his knees from Reagan's clever misrepresentations of his record, which had stuck Ford with a seemingly confused message. Having spent the past few months aggressively touting his conservative credentials, Ford had effectively buried his own broader-minded brand of Republicanism. Pretending to lean further to the right than he actually did may have won him his party's nomination, but voters of all persuasions had seen his act, and many gave it bad reviews. Polls taken at the outset of the 1976 general election campaign showed Ford trailing Carter by thirty points.

Decades later, Ford still bristled about Reagan's decision to challenge him in 1976. To Ford, that action made a hypocrisy out of Reagan's famous Eleventh Commandment: "A Republican should never criticize another Republican." Even though Ford insisted he didn't hold a grudge against Reagan, he clearly did. "I have never publicly criticized Reagan for what he did," Ford recalled. "I can tell you I was shocked when he called me in November of '75 and said he was going to run. I thought, 'What a low-down stunt.' Really burned the hell out of me. I thought I had done a good job and I thought a Reagan challenge would make it more difficult if I won [the nomination], to win the general election. What also irritated me, after I beat him in Kansas City — and I'm the only person who ever beat him in a political race, he never lost another — was that he snubbed me. Put his nose up in the air. After I had defeated him, he only made one appearance on my behalf. And that was at a Republican dinner in Los Angeles, I think. He endorsed me. But in a lukewarm way. There was no question in my mind that if he had campaigned for me in Mississippi, Wisconsin and Missouri, I could have beat Carter. Three or four states were lost by one or two percent. He just wasn't a party player that year. It was all about himself."[25]

After soliciting suggestions from the GOP's leading lights for Nelson Rockefeller's replacement on the ticket, Ford settled on Republican senator Robert J. Dole of Kansas, who was known for his quick wit and strong party fealty. Moreover, pollsters found that Dole "hurt Ford the least among voters," Nessen reported. "He was a true conservative, acceptable to the Reaganites, a hard-hitting campaigner, a friend and supporter of Ford, and a Midwesterner who could appeal to farmers who were angry at the president for imposing a two-month embargo on grain sales to the Soviet Union."[26] At the joint press conference Ford called to announce his vice presidential choice on August 19, Rockefeller gave a particularly gracious endorsement of the ticket he had been forced from.[27]

With the feisty Dole helping out on the hustings, Ford's bid took off. The contest against Jimmy Carter developed into a slugfest, with the Republicans countering the Democrats' charges punch for punch. Yet, true to form, the president accorded his rival the benefit of regular briefings from CIA director George H. W. Bush.[28]

Throughout the Bicentennial Campaign, nobody was cheering Ford on from the sidelines more than Richard Nixon. Exiled at Casa Pacifica, his San Clemente home, Nixon, hoping to repay his friend who campaigned for him in 1960, 1968, and 1972, was hell-bent on returning the favor. Unbeknownst at the time, Nixon was offering Ford both strategic advice and morale boosts from retirement throughout the 1976 campaign. Nixon presented himself in letters as a bruised veteran of political fisticuffs, a California sage with a mobster's instinct for the jugular. On April 22, 1976, he urged Ford to lambaste the Humphrey-Hawkins Bill, which sought to trim unemployment by offering a wide range of public service jobs to citizens willing to take them. To Nixon the bill was a "monstrosity"; calling it "socialism," he recommended, would score points with independent voters.[29] Consistently, Nixon thought, Ford should paint Carter and the Democratic Congress as being soft on communism. "Your 'guts' comment on the Congress' failure to support you on Angola was tops," Nixon wrote Ford on February 12. "You will take a little heat on it — but sometimes the right four letter word is the best way to get a message across."[30]

That August, when Ford was down around 30 percent in the polls, Nixon rallied to his side. In political lore, Nixon was known as a "comeback" artist and now he peppered Ford with his Norman Vincent Peale–like "power of positive thinking" wisdom. "Keep that confident, fighting spirit — and the only poll that matters will come out alright on November 2," Nixon wrote. "The next two months will be the longest and hardest of your life. But I am sure you are ready to give the opposition the fight of their lives."[31]

For a while, Ford did well by stressing his

record in the White House, particularly his efforts to perk up the sagging U.S. economy. On September 13, however, the Labor Department reported that unemployment had risen each of the previous three months, hitting a new high for the year in August. Worse, GNP growth had stalled, the stock market was falling, and inflation was on the rise. This economic news took its toll. Also in September, the president's breathlessly announced program to inoculate every American against a supposedly imminent swine flu epidemic turned disastrous when the vaccine caused temporary paralysis in some recipients and even a few deaths. Soon after that the program became an even bigger joke than Ford's "Whip Inflation Now" initiative, as there was no swine flu epidemic.[32]

With less than two months to go before Election Day, Ford's attempt to campaign on his accomplishments foundered, while Carter took a page from the president's script by casting himself as that rare politician who was actually a decent human being, too. By defining himself as the ultimate post-Watergate Washington outsider, Carter made the case that he was ideally suited to the Augean task of cleaning up after what he called the "Nixon–Ford Administration."[33]

The GOP campaign team pinned its hopes on Ford's performance in the three prime-time debates he had challenged Carter to in quest of free national airtime. The strategy centered on exceeding the public's low expectations of the president, who had the reputation of being a plodding orator, monotonous and awkward. Therefore if he did not fumble a question, if he spoke with grace and certainty, he could score a knockout punch. The first debate, held on September 23 in Philadelphia, focused on economic and domestic issues. Ford acquitted himself well enough to "win" that event, according to various polls taken immediately after the debate, although Carter had certainly scored with his remark that "Mr. Ford, so far as I know, except for avoiding another Watergate, has not accomplished one single major program for this country."[34]

The second debate, on foreign and defense policy, took place October 6 in San Francisco. Trouble arose when panelist Max Frankel of the *New York Times* asked Ford whether détente, particularly as exemplified by the Helsinki Accords, benefited the Soviet Union more than the United States.

Roused to defend the European security conference agreement from the charge that it formalized the Soviet Union's hold over its weaker neighbors, Ford made the astonishing claim that "there is no Soviet domination of Eastern Europe, and there never will be under a Ford Administration."[35]

All of his campaign staff's best efforts to make him look smart and presidential over the past few months faded to naught the instant Ford made the remark. What he had said was so patently wrong that it made the president of the United States look truly stupid — and nearly a hundred million Americans had watched him say it live on TV. Even worse, when Frankel gave him the opportunity to retreat from his statement, Ford instead dug himself into an even deeper hole. Asserting that he did not believe that the Yugoslavs, Romanians, or Poles "consider themselves dominated by the Soviet Union," Ford pointed out — laughably — that "each of those countries is independent, autonomous; it has its own territorial integrity. And the United States does not concede that those countries are under the domination of the Soviet Union." Carter naturally pounced on the amazing gift just handed him, sniffing: "I would like to see Mr. Ford convince the Polish-

Americans and the Czech-Americans and the Hungarian-Americans in this country . . . that those countries don't live under the domination and supervision of the Soviet Union behind the Iron Curtain."[36]

Ford was forced to spend the next few days clumsily trying to explain what he had meant — that the United States did not accept the legitimacy of the Soviets' domination of Eastern Europe — but there was no way to gloss over the utter dumbness of his original statement, as the president would eventually acknowledge. *National Review*'s editor in chief, William F. Buckley Jr., dubbed Ford's gaffe "the ultimate Polish joke."[37]

As the president scrambled to correct the perception that he was really dumb, Bob Dole set off charges that he was just plain mean. On October 15, during the one nationally televised vice presidential debate, Dole dismayed many viewers by calling World Wars I and II as well as the Korean conflict "Democrat wars." Making matters worse, he continued, "I figured it up the other day, we added up the killed and wounded. . . . In Democrat wars in this century it would be 1.6 million Americans, enough to fill the city of Detroit."[38] Many voters took exception to that harsh a degree of partisanship, and would show their disapproval at the polls. The final presidential debate barely registered in the news after these Republican flubs.

On October 30, while en route aboard Air Force One from a last-minute campaign stop in Houston to another in Philadelphia, President Ford videotaped a final pitch to the American people, to be broadcast nationwide the night before the election. After laying out the grim situation he had inherited from the horrors of Richard Nixon just twenty-seven months before, Ford boasted that since then, "America has turned around. I put the Ship of State on an even keel. I held a firm hand on the tiller for a steady course. Today, we are doing much, much better. The rate of inflation has been cut by more than 50 percent. . . . We have added 4 million more jobs in the last 18 months. . . . We have restored confidence and trust in the White House itself, and America is at peace."

On the eve of the election the final voter surveys showed a statistically tied race. Carter led by a point in the last Harris poll; Gallup's final tally put Ford up by the same margin, marking the first time in the race that the president had come out on top in any poll.[39] For all its troubles, in just over two months the Republican ticket had staged a twenty-nine-point comeback.

But it wasn't enough. Although Ford took all of the West along with the core of the Midwest, Carter captured not only most of the South but enough of the Eastern states — including New York, by a notable margin — to win the 1976 election. In the popular vote, Carter notched 40.8 million votes to Ford's 39.1 million. The electoral college tally of 297 to 240 (with one vote going to Ronald Reagan) marked the closest presidential contest since 1916.[40]

A couple of hours after he sent his official telegram to Jimmy Carter conceding the election, President Ford resorted to the lingo of his favorite sport to commend his senior staff for their valiant failed efforts. "I want to thank everybody for their service, both in the campaign and to the nation," he told the aides gathered in the Roosevelt Room in a stress-hoarsened quaver. "We took the ball right down to the goal line, but we couldn't get it over. We gave it a hell of a shot. We have nothing to be ashamed of. We should all be very proud."[41] The *New York Times* agreed, proclaiming in a postelection editorial that "Mr. Ford today enjoys the respect and affection of his fellow citizens. Moreover, he leaves the country in better shape than he found it."[42]

Yet Ford himself was profoundly disappointed by his narrow defeat. He wasn't used to coming up short in the eyes of the public, and he had truly enjoyed being president. To lose out on a full term of his own, and by such a slim margin, inevitably led him to second-guess his every move. He pored over the whole litany of what-ifs, rationalizing the loss to his own mind by endlessly reviewing every harm he had done to his campaign, from pardoning Nixon to dumping Rockefeller to muffing the Eastern Europe issue on live TV. "And what if Reagan had been able to put aside his own disappointment and campaign more enthusiastically for me?" Ford would wonder in his memoir.[43]

After losing, Ford's first instinct was to pray for his country's future. Although he never wore it on his sleeve, Ford's deep Christian faith provided the backbone to his life. The Fords went to church most Sundays, without fanfare. And privately, they befriended Reverend Billy Graham. Upon losing to Carter, Ford prayed for his Democrat opponent, knowing full well the dangerous Cold War issues he would inherit. Unusual for a politician, Ford was practically egoless, a character trait that Graham embraced. "During the election period I prayed constantly that 'God's Will' be done," Graham wrote Ford a couple weeks after Election Day. "This was the prayer of Jesus the night before the cross. He said, 'Not my will but Thine be done.' For some mysterious reason unknown to us Mr. Carter won. You and your associates put on a whale of a campaign. With the low Republican registration in the country I think Mr. Carter should be asking himself how he came so close to losing."[44]

Historians looking for a shorthand summarization of Ford's White House tenure don't have to look any further than his final State of the Union address. In an emotional good-bye, Ford told Congress and the American people on January 12, 1977: "I can report that the state of the Union is good. There is room for improvement, as always, but today we have a more perfect Union than when my stewardship began."[45]

Eight days later, on January 20, Gerald Ford was seated next to Jimmy Carter on a platform above the U.S. Capitol's front steps when the new leader of the free world took the podium to deliver his inaugural address. Carter's first words would surprise and deeply touch the man he was replacing. "For myself and for our nation," the new president began, "I want to thank my predecessor for all he has done to heal our land." Ford was shocked at Carter's generosity, and from that Inauguration Day onward a genuine friendship slowly developed between them.

Jerry and Betty Ford hugged dozens of Washington friends they had made during their twenty-eight years living along the Potomac River. They then got on board the Marine One helicopter, which was supposed to take them directly to Andrews Air Force Base. From there it was on to Houston, where Ford would give his first speech as an ex-president, at a gala celebrating the legacy of the football coach Vince Lombardi. Then they would head to Rancho Mirage, California, just outside of Palm Springs, for what they hoped would be a happy retirement. But once Marine One took off, Ford had an abrupt request. He asked the pilot to fly around the Capitol, not the White House. "That's my real home," he said, gazing out the window, eyes filled with tears.[46]

From the moment Ford left the White House, that valediction that he had "healed" America would remain the most enduring legacy of his term in office, though hardly the only one. For it was Gerald R. Ford who dissipated the pall of Richard Nixon, however controversially, and who shepherded the nation safely through to the end of its most divisive war while living up to the United States's ensuing responsibilities to South Vietnam's refugees. It was Ford whose help in forging the Helsinki Accords opened the way for the collapse of Soviet communism. It was Ford who acknowledged the seriousness of the global energy crisis and who conveyed the urgent need for cooperation to do something about it to the rest of the industrialized world, and whose careful fiscal policies cut inflation in half and boosted the U.S. economy out of its direst fix since the Great Depression. And it was Ford who, purely by dint of coming across as a really nice, normal guy, restored Americans' faith in the validity of their government.

In Henry Kissinger's view, "Ford's lack of guile became a part of the healing process" after Vietnam and Watergate. "He carried off one of the most complex assumptions of authority with such apparent ease, and he established his brand of leadership at home and abroad with such remarkable speed, that it came to be forgotten how close to chaos Watergate had brought us."[47] In the end, Kissinger concluded, "Other Presidents were to receive the credit for winning the Cold War. But I am certain the time will come when it is recognized that the Cold War could not have been won had not Gerald Ford, at a tragic period of America's history, been there to keep us from losing it."[48]

Pundits often wondered how Ford got along so keenly with the supersized ego of Henry Kissinger. Always comfortable in his own skin, Ford preferred surrounding himself with intellectuals and policy experts who could help him lead effectively. His motto was: the more bright candles in the room, the better.

While Kissinger worked in around-the-clock crisis mode, an aura of calmness usually shrouded Ford. He avoided stress, operating well in a crisis, and had nerves of steel. And humor was a constant factor in his daily regiment; he always refused to take himself too seriously. Unlike most of his White House predecessors, Ford, the so-called accidental president, wasn't warped by raw ambition. He exuded a laissez-faire attitude toward his own destiny. He was never consumed with being president. He simply didn't lose sleep fretting over what history would say about him. This doesn't mean, however, that he was the personification of virtue — he had shortcomings. He didn't grasp, until it was too late, that the art of persuasion was the true essence of the modern presidency.

Throughout his 896 days in the White House, it seemed that Ford, the veteran congressman from Michigan's Fifth District, didn't fully comprehend the massive executive power at his disposal. He behaved more like a Grand Rapids Rotarian leader or Capitol Hill lobbyist than Theodore Roosevelt in the bully pulpit. But you could never accuse him of being a legacy monger. Ford believed he had an obligation to history but history had no obligation to him. Imbued with a Trumanesque do-the-right-thing attitude, Ford was an Eagle Scout, always clinging to the three rules drummed into his head as a Michigan kid: Tell the Truth, Work Hard, and Come to Dinner on Time. That wasn't a sophisticated philosophy, but he wasn't that sophisticated a guy. But he was honest. No matter the day or season, Ford always had the courage of his convictions, the courage to change his mind, to say, "I was wrong."

Often historians want to label politicians, demarcating them as a New Dealer, a neocon, or some such moniker. Ford was difficult to pin down in such a limiting fashion.

He was always a Midwest conservative with a healthy skepticism about the power of government to fundamentally change people's lives for the better. Throughout his political career he would reflexively ask whenever a new bill or program was proposed: What's it gonna cost? Who's gonna benefit? How many people is it gonna require? It is gonna infringe on the private sector? But consistent with that was his libertarian belief that the government should stay out of the boardroom, the classroom, and the bedroom. He was mystified by the aggressive social conservatives who openly denounced government yet were perfectly willing to use government in order to pursue their fundamentalist Christian agenda. Ford was a "Leave Me Alone Conservative," albeit with a deep Lincolnian streak, particularly on civil rights. It was not a simple formulation, but he was consistent in his beliefs.

Nothing, in fact, infuriated Ford more than lying. He was generally shocked that Richard Nixon, a friend for decades, would baldly lie to him about his involvement in Watergate. (He was doubly shocked that Nixon would use Julie, his own daughter, to lie for him.) And Ford wasn't like other politicians in another singular regard: he wouldn't gossip. He thought it poisoned the soul. He always tried to see the good in everyone. Only twice did the historian Richard Norton Smith, a close friend and speechwriter to the ex-president, ever hear Ford make disparaging remarks about people. "The worst he would say about someone was, 'He's a bad man,' " Smith recalled. "Coming from Ford that's the ultimate insult. The only two men he said that about were John Dean and Gordon Liddy. Nicely balanced, that's typical Ford."[49]

His ability not to hate or hold grudges won him fans. An unexpected endorsement of Ford's character, for example, came from Benjamin C. Bradlee, the longtime executive editor of the *Washington Post.* "In the story conference room on the news floor of *The Washington Post,*" Bradlee wrote in his memoir, *A Good Life,* "hangs a large framed color photograph of a smiling President Ford, superimposed with the caption: 'I got my job through *The Washington Post.*' " The *Post's* Watergate coverage, of course, had brought down the Nixon presidency. Ford signed this poster "To Ben Bradlee and all my friends at *The Washington Post* . . . Jerry Ford." Bradlee added, admiringly, "I can't think of another president who would have done the same thing."[50]

Most Americans, in fact, agreed with the Reverend Billy Graham, who matter-of-factly wrote that Ford had been "the right man at the right time to lead this nation."[51]

Perhaps the most poignant encomium on Ford's presidency came from the *Post's* gentlemanly political correspondent David S. Broder, who wrote shortly after the 1976 election, "In an odd, inexplicable way . . . the truth has begun to dawn on people in the final days of Gerald R. Ford's tenure that he was the kind of President Americans wanted — and didn't know they had."[52]

11
RETIREMENT DECADES

On January 3, 1977, Richard Nixon, who was working on his memoir, *RN,* the first of seven books he'd write as an ex-president, sent a letter to the White House aimed at jump-starting Ford's sagging morale. "As your years in public office draw to a close," Nixon wrote, "I thought you might find it heartwarming to reflect on the theme of a little rhyme I can across recently in my book research." The inspiring verse came from Robert Farnon's *Tough at the Top,* a Broadway musical from 1949, when Ford and Nixon first became congressional colleagues and friends. "This is not the end this is but a beginning," Nixon wrote in longhand. "When the fight is lost/there's a fight worth winning/Nothing is wasted, nothing is in vain/the seas roll over but the rocks remain."[1]

While much has been made of the special friendship Ford developed with Carter once both men left the White House, the odd role Nixon continued to play in his pardoner's life has been neglected. Essentially, whenever Ford (or his wife, Betty) got criticized in the press, Nixon rose to his defense. A case in point is when Ford's former press secretary, Ron Nessen, wrote a memoir that disparaged Betty Ford as having a serious alcohol problem. "I thought Ron Nessen's comments on Betty were contemptible," Nixon wrote Ford on May 14, 1978. "Tell Betty her *many* friends won't believe him. And for her few enemies: The hell with them."[2]

The most pressing concern the Fords confronted in their first year out of the White House was financial solvency. All their years in public service had left the Fords cash strapped. In March, both Jerry and Betty signed lucrative publishing contracts for their memoirs, *A Time to Heal* and *The Times of My Life.* That same month Ford returned to the White House for the first time since leaving office, discussing the Middle East, the Panama Canal, and other issues with President Carter. The combination of this visit, plus reliving his days in power while writing his memoir, made Ford, at fleeting moments, want to get back into the political fray. In the fall of 1978

Ford even flirted with the idea of running for president again. "It definitely crossed my mind," he recalled. "Carter wasn't doing well and I'd already proven that I could beat Reagan. There was an opening but I passed. We were enjoying our life out here in the desert and I was just starting to make some money."[3]

Amid widespread press speculation that he would run, Ford pulled the plug on the notion on March 16, 1980. "America needs a new President," he said. "I have determined that I can best help that cause by not being a candidate for President, which might further divide my party."[4] But the name Gerald Ford still had magic to it. As Americans grew weary of Carter's double-digit inflation, long gasoline lines, and terminal Iranian hostage crisis, there was a longing for the pipe puffer from Michigan. At the Republican National Convention in Detroit, in fact, representatives from Ronald Reagan and Gerald Ford attempted to work out the details of having Ford on the ticket as Reagan's vice presidential nominee. CBS news anchor Walter Cronkite called the potential team-up a "co-presidency"; however, it never happened.[5] Always the loyal Republican, Ford contented himself stumping for Reagan across America. On the

Sunday before the election, Ford appeared on NBC's *Meet the Press* criticizing Carter for his handling of the Iranian hostage debacle. "Believe me," Ford said. "Ronnie and I had our differences. But I thought he would be better than Carter."[6]

Reagan, of course, won and Ford grew content raising money for his Presidential Library in Ann Arbor and his Presidential Museum in Grand Rapids. Unlike all the other presidents since Herbert Hoover, Ford opened two separate facilities in his name to be administered by the National Archives. (The museum was more of a shrine, while his government papers were housed at his alma mater. Both edifices opened in 1981.)

A tragedy in the Middle East brought Ford back to center stage that autumn. On October 6, 1981, Egyptian president Anwar Sadat was killed, gunned down in a hail of automatic gunfire at a military parade in Cairo that left eleven dead and forty wounded. In *A Time to Heal* Ford had written about Sadat in glowing terms, describing him as a combination of a "professional soldier's erect posture with an aristocratic air of elegance."[7] Both men enjoyed lighting up a pipe while they spoke. As president, Ford learned three fundamental imperatives about negotiating with Sadat that all worked in America's favor: he never lied, he desperately wanted to avoid a confrontation between Egypt and Israel in the Sinai Peninsula, and he disdained the bullying tactics of the Soviet Union. Without the diplomatic spade work conducted by Ford and Kissinger from 1974 to 1977, President Jimmy Carter would never have been successful at Camp David in brokering the historic peace accords between Egypt and Israel in 1979.

It was at Sadat's funeral that Ford and Carter, old political adversaries, deepened their friendship. An easy camaraderie developed between the two ex-presidents, sustained in the coming years as their wives, Rosalyn and Betty, also grew close, lobbying together on such worthwhile causes as alcohol and drug prevention, the Equal Rights Ammendment, and health care policies toward the mentally ill. "On foreign policy our views are similar," Ford recalled in 1995, "so we can work together on joint projects very effectively."[8]

On the long flight back from the funeral, Carter accepted Ford's offer to cohost an upcoming two-day conference at his presidential library in Ann Arbor; in turn, Ford offered to cochair Carter Center programs in Atlanta. Later, they coauthored articles in leading periodicals and issued numerous joint statements. But mostly they worked together on issues pertaining to the Middle East peace process.[9] The Carter-Ford team, in fact, made international news in 1981 by boldly stating that the United States had to start talking with the Palestine Liberation Organization if any meaningful peace settlement was to be reached in the Middle East. "We thought it was wrong to label Palestinians as terrorists," Ford recalled. "We would have to start negotiations with the PLO if peace was going to be achieved. A precondition, of course, was the PLO recognizing Israel's right to exist."[10]

While on the surface it looked as if the Fords had the ideal retirement lifestyle going, in truth they were grappling with household dysfunction. Ever since her bout with breast cancer, Betty Ford had struggled with alcohol and pill addiction. Eventually, through the loving intervention of her family, she enrolled in a chemical dependency program at the Naval Hospital in Long Beach, California. Jerry understood that only one out of ten marriages survived an alcoholic wife, and he immediately came to Betty's bedside. He visited her regularly in Long Beach, gave up drinking his scotch, and helped her launch a modern detox center — The Betty Ford Clinic — in Palm Springs. The Fords, along with their neighbor Leonard Firestone, himself a recovering alcoholic, opened the world-class treatment facility at the Eisenhower Medical Center on October 3, 1982. "We're proud of you, Mom," Ford said at the podium, fighting tears. "We want you to know that we love you."[11]

Throughout the 1980s, Ford's name would appear in newspaper articles pertaining to the number of corporate boards he sat on. According to the historian Mark K. Updegrove, he signed on with Amax, Inc.; American Express Company; Shearson/American Express; Santa Fe International Corporation; Texas Commerce Bank; Tiger International, Inc.; Beneficial Corporation of New Jersey; and 20th Century Fox Film Corporation.[12] He caught some squawks for "being greedy" or "selling out" to corporate America. While Ford was collecting his one-hundred-thousand-dollar-a-year government pension, he netted more than a million dollars in supplemental income from these corporations. "I'm a private citizen now" was Ford's answer to the carping. "It's nobody's business."[13]

What saved Ford from damaging his integrity was, ironically, his sense of humor.

Instead of being angry at Chevy Chase, they became good friends. Against everybody's advice, Ford, along with Henry Kissinger, gave a cameo performance on the ABC soap opera *Dynasty.* In 1986 he hosted a symposium on "Humor and the Presidency" and a year later published a book on the topic. And at a 1989 conference on his presidency at Hofstra University, Ford seemed to enjoy poking fun at himself, our most athletic president who had been portrayed in history as a stumbler.[14] Hofstra published two volumes of scholarly papers from the symposium with the net effect of giving Ford's presidency a big thumbs-up.

The true opening salvo of Ford revisionism was fired by the veteran journalist Richard Reeves in a December 1996 article for *American Heritage* titled, "I'm Sorry, Mr. President." Reeves apologized for having written a highly critical book in 1975 titled *A Ford, Not a Lincoln,* in which he called Ford "slow," "unimaginative," and "not very articulate." But now, two decades later, Reeves revisited his bestseller and found it wrong-minded. Even though Reeves clung to his thesis that Alexander Haig had secretly brokered the pardon, he now believed that Ford's pardon had been right. "Whatever his failings as a leader," Reeves wrote of Ford, "and there were many, he was right about the big one."[15] When the article appeared, Reeves had just published an acclaimed biography of John F. Kennedy and was deemed one of the top "presidential historians" working the circuit. "I was grateful that Reeves had the guts to apologize," Ford recalled. "Most journalists don't do that. His article confirmed my belief that history would judge the pardon favorably. It just took time for people to get to that conclusion . . . a couple of decades."[16]

Just a few months after the Reeves article appeared, Bob Woodward began researching the Nixon pardon for his book *Shadow: Five Presidents and the Legacy of Watergate*. On September 22, 1997, Woodward interviewed the eighty-four-year-old former president for the first time. They met at the Waldorf Towers in New York City. Ford admitted that Haig had offered a deal, but he had declined it. "Yes, on paper, without action it was a deal," he said, "but it never became a deal because I never accepted." Woodward conducted a follow-up interview with Ford in Rancho Mirage eight months later. This time he focused on why Ford hadn't pressed Nixon to admit his guilt publicly. It was a good question, and Ford had a ready answer. The ex-president pulled out his wallet and fumbled for his frayed clipping about the 1915 *Burdick v. United States* Supreme Court decision. He handed it to Woodward to read. Dutifully, the veteran reporter did, slowing down for the key phrase, "Most important, the justices found that a pardon carried an imputation of guilt, acceptance, a confession of it."

Ford beamed. Hearing that legal phrase caused him to interject that according to the 1915 decision, Nixon, by accepting the pardon, *had* admitted guilt in the Watergate cover-up. "That was," Ford told Woodward, "very reassuring to me."

All great reporters have what Hemingway called "built-in bullshit detectors," and Woodward was surely no exception. He emerged from his interviews with Ford convinced that the pardon was not just justified but was downright heroic. "Ford was wise to act," was Woodward's conclusion. "What at first and perhaps for many years looked like a decision to protect Nixon was instead largely designed to protect the nation. Watergate was a poison that would not go away. There was more to it than I saw at the time. Over the years the periodic release of new Nixon tapes shows new criminality and smallness. Ford wanted to protect his presidency, a proper goal because the president is an extension of the nation. The only way out of the Watergate atmosphere was to move fast, to short-circuit the process. Preoccupation with Nixon's fate could have continued for years."[17]

Winning over journalistic kingpins like Reeves and Woodward did not happen by chance. Quietly, but with great determination, Ford always stuck to his guns, insisting the pardon was a national necessity. But Ford, as ex-president, had made it a policy to treat even his critics with uncommon graciousness. His body language exuded kindness and honesty. There were no equivocations or downcast eyes. Any street-smart cop interrogating Ford would have reached the same conclusion: this man had nothing to hide. Besides exuding integrity, Ford appealed to liberals in the media because he disagreed with GOP conservatives on such social issues as affirmative action, gun control, abortion, and gay rights. Liberals who abhorred the Reagan Revolution were more willing to embrace Ford's unthreatening Republican centrism. In a 2003 interview, Ford deemed his standing up to the Republican Right his greatest lifetime achievement. "My wife and I are moderate Republicans," Ford said. "We are pro-choice and speak out openly on that.

We understand people who have different views who are opposed to abortion, but I don't think the hard right wing of the Republican Party can get re-elected with any candidate against *Roe v. Wade.* I think the party has to have somebody in the middle who invites people from both the left and right. And I illustrate this by showing that when the Democrats were recognized as left-wing liberal, they didn't win anything. Mondale, Dukakis, moving down the list. Only when Clinton came along and talked a good moderate game, did they win. I'm not ashamed to be called a centrist. I'm proud."[18]

Oddly, it was Ford's defense of Bill Clinton in late 1998 that further endeared him to the left. Although President Clinton's lewd behavior during the Lewinsky affair — particularly lying to the American people — offended Ford, he thought impeachment was a mistake. Instead of staying quiet, on October 3, 1998, the eighty-five-year-old Ford wrote an op-ed piece for the *New York Times* recommending that Clinton be "rebuked" in Congress but not impeached. He framed it as a compromise.[19] Written as the House Judiciary Committee prepared to evaluate the ten-thousand-page Starr Report and then determine Clinton's fate, the op-ed was quickly embraced by Democrats. While Clintonians didn't cotton to the rebuke idea, they fully agreed with Ford's position that GOP politicians were witch-hunting the president to the detriment of the nation. "Gerald Ford is a man who has been there, who understands a situation like this and understands the importance of deferring to Constitutional standards under all circumstances," Gregory Craig, the special counsel to the president, told the *Times.* "President Ford is absolutely right: this kind of conduct simply doesn't rise to the level of impeachable offense." Overnight, Ford became a hero of the Left.[20]

Shortly before Christmas, in a second *Times* op-ed, Ford and Jimmy Carter promoted the idea of a Senate "censure" of the president.[21] The former presidents were, in essence, pleading the case of reasonable punishment for Clinton. They wanted his ears boxed, but they didn't want to see him driven from the White House. Republicans, like Congressman Tom DeLay of Texas, were furious at Ford, deeming him a turncoat. "DeLay wrote me the nastiest letter imaginable," Ford recalled. "He was downright rude. But I didn't care. I thought the House impeachment was enough. If I could pardon Nixon then we could certainly censure — not impeach — Clinton in the Senate. It was the centrist position. And it's what was right for the country."[22]

For his entire public life, Ford had warred with the Republican Right — things didn't change just because he was an octogenarian. Conservatives were infuriated, for example, when Ford, once again using the *New York Times* op-ed page as his forum, defended affirmative action as a legitimate criterion for admission to the University of Michigan. Right-wing talk radio lit into Ford as being soft-skulled, a buffoon. This animosity only grew when, on August 11, 1999, President Clinton praised Ford and awarded him the Presidential Medal of Freedom. When in the 2000 presidential election, George W. Bush squeaked out a victory over Al Gore among widespread reports of voter fraud in Florida, Ford publicly worried about the state of American democracy. He couldn't celebrate a GOP victory when voter disenfranchisement might have occurred. Instead of merely worrying about it, Ford took direct action, joining forces with Carter as cochairs of the National Commission on Federal Election Reform.

All of these events were a buildup to what Ford considered the most redemptive honor of his life. Every year, the John F. Kennedy Foundation announces winners of the "Profile in Courage Award," given to elected officials who "withstood strong opposition from constituents, powerful interest groups or adversaries to follow what she or he believes is the right course of action." In April 2001 the award went to Gerald Ford for his controversial decision to pardon Richard Nixon. When the announcement appeared in newspapers, veterans of the Watergate wars rubbed their eyes in disbelief. After all, Senator Ted Kennedy, who was slated to present the award at a ceremony, had denounced Ford for the pardon vociferously back in 1974. Like many Americans, however, Kennedy had come full circle. "I was one of those who spoke out against his action then," Kennedy explained. "But time has a way of clarifying past events, and now we see that President Ford was right."[23]

The biggest promoter of Ford winning the award was Caroline Kennedy, daughter of the thirty-fifth president. She had recently visited the Ford Library and her gracious tour guide was President Ford himself. "For me it was especially meaningful to hear stories of other times," she wrote in a thank-you note, "and people I have heard about all my life."[24] She had been touched by Ford's soft-spoken Kent County charm. Another award advocate was the Pulitzer Prize–winning historian David McCullough, who had spoken at the Ford Museum in Grand Rapids a couple of times. He had grown extremely fond of the ex-president. When the prize committee debated who deserved the 2001 award, McCullough threw his support wholeheartedly behind Ford. It proved to be an inspired choice. The story of the Kennedys thanking Ford for pardoning Nixon led the news. Letters came pouring in praising the surprise choice. "I am glad they finally caught up with the courage and wisdom required to grant Nixon a pardon when you did," Notre Dame president Theodore Hesburgh wrote Ford. "The Kennedy Award says a good deal and all of it is vindicating the wisdom of your action at a difficult time."[25] James Callaghan, the former British prime minister, wrote Ford that the award had inspired the press to "re-evaluate your presidency and recall what a good president you were, at a time of the greatest difficulty in the United States."[26]

Four months later, the 9/11 terrorist attacks took place. A stunned Ford headed to Washington, D.C., to help salve the nation's despair. On September 14, Jerry and Betty, holding hands, attended the National Day of Prayer and Remembrance ceremony at the National Cathedral. "That day I just cried and cried," Ford recalled. "Those poor, poor people. Our poor, poor country."[27]

Ford had transcended being the "accidental" or "pardon" president; he was now seen as America's bipartisan, elder statesman "healer." Even former enemies treated him with reverence. Honors came raining down on Ford from all corners; for example, the National Collegiate Athletic Association created an annual leadership award in his name while the National Archives hosted a symposium to honor his public service achievements. Simply put, Ford had become beloved.

On November 12, 2006, it was safe to say that Ford's stubbornness, his insistence that the Nixon pardon was a national imperative, had won converts. He was now, at age ninety-three, the oldest president in American history, having surpassed Ronald Reagan. It had taken over thirty-five years, but a historical revisionism had firmly taken root. History was starting to congeal in Ford's favor. A consensus was emerging that the Nixon pardon was the right thing to do.

The end, however, was nearing for Ford. His health was failing terribly. Twice that year he had been hospitalized for heart problems. Given his precarious health, detailed plans were adopted for his funeral, which, unlike Reagan's state funeral with all the pomp, would be low-keyed and Trumanesque. There would be, for example, no horse-drawn procession through the streets of Washington. Just simple ceremonies at St. Margaret's Episcopal Church in Palm Desert, California, and at the National Cathedral, followed by a service in his hometown of Grand Rapids, where he'd be buried. His longtime political aide Bob Hartmann had already been asked to be a pallbearer, as had his former chiefs of staff Donald Rumsfeld and Dick Cheney.

Gerald Ford died on December 26, 2006, at his home in Rancho Mirage, California. His obituary ran for three full pages in the *New York Times.* The word used over and over again by commentators analyzing what his life meant was "healer." His wife, Betty, issued a simple statement, saying that Ford's life had been "filled with love of God, his family, and his country." Old photographs of him playing football at the University of Michigan were flashed around the world on cable television. The photographer David Hume Kennerly spoke for many when he noted that Ford had the "least guile" of anybody he ever met. "There were no 'two Gerald Fords,' " Kennerly said. "There was no other agenda, no secret life."[28]

When the thirty-eighth president was brought back to Washington for the last time, his motorcade stopped briefly at the World War II Memorial, where members of the armed services and a contingent of Eagle Scouts paid tribute to him. To honor Ford's long service in Congress, his body lay in state not only in the Capitol rotunda but also at the doors of both the House of Representatives and the Senate. Over the course of the New Year's weekend, thousands of Americans lined up to pay tribute to him, and Ford's children greeted many of them personally. On New Year's Day, the members of the University of Michigan football team wore a patch with the number 48, Ford's jersey number, in tribute to him. At the service at the National Cathedral, former president George H. W. Bush said that Gerald Ford was "a Norman Rockwell painting come to life," and Henry Kissinger said that knowing Ford was a "badge of honor." There was a lighthearted aspect to the service, with Tom Brokaw recalling the ugly plaids that Ford would wear. But, mainly, everyone was focused on Betty Ford and the fifty-eight years of marriage she had shared with her husband.

Even the *New York Times* editorial page, long a critic of the Nixon pardon, praised other aspects of Ford's character so heartily that it bordered on hagiography. "Mr. Ford deserves to be remembered for more than the pardon," the *Times* said. "Marking the end of a national nightmare is no small thing."[29] And if the public outpouring of affection for Ford was any indication, he had risen to the rank of "near-great president" in the minds of many Americans. The long healing process was finally complete.

NOTES

1: Michigan Upbringing

1. Author interview with Gerald Ford, Rancho Mirage, Calif., March 23, 2003.
2. James M. Cannon, "Gerald R. Ford: Minority Leader of the House of Representatives, 1965–1973," in Roger H. Davidson, Susan Webb Hammond, and Raymond W. Smock, eds., *Masters of the House* (Boulder, Colo.: Westview Press, 1998), p. 261.
3. Julian Street, *Abroad at Home* (New York: Century, 1916), p. 128.
4. David A. Horrocks and William H. McNitt, "Gerald R. Ford Biography," *Guide to Historical Materials in the Gerald R. Ford Library* (Ann Arbor, Mich.: Gerald R. Ford Library, 2003), p. 1.
5. President Gerald R. Ford, in a speech before the National Quadrennial Convention of the Polish-American Congress in

Philadelphia, Penn., September 24, 1976. Transcript appears in *The Presidential Campaign 1976, Volume Two, Part Two: Gerald R. Ford* (Washington, D.C.: U.S. Government Printing Office, 1979), p. 754.

6. Jerald F. terHorst, *Gerald Ford and the Future of the Presidency* (New York: Third Press, 1974), pp. 38–40. In 1929 and 1930, young Jerry Ford earned two dollars (plus lunches) a week, working at Bill Skougis's restaurant across the street from South High every school day from 11:30 a.m. to 1 p.m. and from 7 to 10 p.m. one night a week.

7. James Cannon, *Time and Chance: Gerald Ford's Appointment with History: 1913–1974* (New York: HarperCollins, 1994), pp. 4–26.

8. Ibid., pp. 12–13.

9. President Gerald R. Ford, in remarks at a Michigan Union dinner for the University of Michigan football team and athletic staff, Ann Arbor, Michigan, September 15, 1976. Transcript appears in *The Presidential Campaign 1976, Volume Two, Part Two: Gerald R. Ford,* pp. 742–43.

10. terHorst, *Gerald Ford and the Future of the Presidency,* p. 40.

11. Ibid, p. 42.
12. Ibid., pp. 42–43.
13. Author interview with Gerald Ford, Ann Arbor, Mich., April 18, 2000.
14. Israel Shenker, "Ford, a Traditionalist Who Believes in Home, Family, Hard Work, and Patriotism," *New York Times,* August 9, 1974, p. 8.
15. terHorst, *Gerald Ford and the Future of the Presidency,* pp. 8–9.
16. Robert Drury and Tom Clavin, "How Lieutenant Ford Saved His Ship," *New York Times,* December 28, 2006.
17. Cannon, *Time and Chance,* pp. 37–38.
18. Ibid., p. 11.
19. *President Ford: The Man and His Record* (Washington, D.C.: Congressional Quarterly, 1974), p. 32.
20. Author interview with Gerald Ford, Rancho Mirage, Calif., March 23, 2003.

2: Man of the House

1. terHorst, *Gerald Ford and the Future of the Presidency,* p. 53.
2. Bud Vestal, *Jerry Ford, Up Close: An Investigative Biography* (New York: Coward, McCann & Geoghegan, 1974), p. 100.
3. Author interview with Gerald Ford, Ran-

cho Mirage, Calif., March 23, 2003.

4. Cannon, *Time and Chance,* p. 53.

5. Richard Nixon to Gerald Ford, January 27, 1994, Gerald R. Ford Personal Papers, New York, N.Y.

6. Author interview with Gerald Ford, Rancho Mirage, Calif., March 23, 2003.

7. Ibid.

8. Ibid.

9. Ibid.

10. Richard Nixon to Gerald Ford, June 28, 1993, Gerald R. Ford Personal Papers, New York, N.Y.

11. terHorst, *Gerald Ford and the Future of the Presidency,* pp. 56, 56n.

12. Gerald R. Ford, *A Time to Heal* (New York: Harper & Row, 1979), p. 68.

13. "G.O.P. Group Seeks to Unseat Martin as House Leader," *New York Times,* January 6, 1959, p. 1.

14. Ivan Hinderaker, "The 1960 Republican Convention: Chicago and Before," in Paul Tillett, ed., *Inside Politics: The National Conventions, 1960* (New Brunswick, N.J.: Rutgers University Press, 1962), p. 21.

15. "Favorite Son Chosen," *New York Times,* April 24, 1960, p. 76.

16. Remarks delivered by former president Gerald R. Ford at the Profile in Courage Award Ceremony, May 21, 2001.

17. Robert L. Peabody, *The Ford-Halleck Minority Leadership Contest, 1965* (New York: McGraw-Hill, 1966), p. 4.

18. "Ten Who Lead in Congress," *New York Times Magazine,* May 5, 1963, p. 18.

19. "Johnson Names a 7-Man Panel to Investigate Assassination," *New York Times,* November 30, 1963, p. 1.

20. Author interview with Gerald Ford, Rancho Mirage, Calif., March 23, 2003.

21. Ford, *A Time to Heal,* pp. 74–75.

22. *The Warren Report* (The Associated Press, [1964]), p. 12.

23. Gerald R. Ford and John R. Stiles, *Portrait of the Assassin* (New York: Simon & Schuster, 1965).

24. Gerald R. Ford, interviewed on CBS-TV's *Face the Nation,* aired June 6, 1976. A transcript appears in *The Presidential Campaign 1976, Volume Two, Part One: Gerald R. Ford,* pp. 572–75.

25. Author interview with Gerald Ford, Rancho Mirage, Calif., March 23, 2003.

26. Gerald R. Ford, "What Can Save the G.O.P.?" *Fortune,* January 1965, p. 110.

27. Ibid., pp. 110–11.

28. James B. Reston, "The Struggle for Leadership in the Republican Party," *New York Times,* December 18, 1964, p. 32.

29. "Burch Urges G.O.P. to End Squabbling," *New York Times*, January 5, 1965, p. 18.
30. Don Oberdorfer, "He Wants to Be Speaker of the House," *New York Times Magazine*, April 30, 1967.
31. "Vietnam II: A Dilemma for Both Parties," *New York Times*, May 7, 1967, p. 219.

3: Foot Soldier for Nixon

1. Donald Tacheron and Morris Udall, *The Job of the Congressman* (Indianapolis: Bobbs-Merrill, 1970), p. 66.
2. terHorst, *Gerald Ford and the Future of the Presidency*, p. 97.
3. Randall B. Ripley, *Party Leaders in the House of Representatives* (Washington, D.C.: Brookings Institution Press, 1967), p. 46.
4. Richard Reeves, *A Ford, Not a Lincoln* (New York: Harcourt Brace Jovanovich, 1975), pp. 15–16.
5. John W. Kingdon, *Congressmen's Voting Decisions* (New York: Harper & Row, 1981), p. 128.
6. Richard Bolling, *Power in the House* (New York: Capricorn Books, 1968), p. 18.

7. *President Ford: The Man and His Record* (Washington, D.C.: Congressional Quarterly, 1974), p. 28.

8. Ford, *A Time to Heal,* p. 85.

9. Richard M. Nixon, *RN: The Memoirs of Richard Nixon* (New York: Grosset & Dunlap, 1978), p. 312.

10. Ford, *A Time to Heal,* p. 86.

11. David Wallechinsky, *David Wallechinsky's Twentieth Century: History with the Boring Parts Left Out* (New York: Little, Brown and Company, 1995), p. 68.

12. Nixon, *RN,* p. 414.

13. John D. Ehrlichman, *Witness to Power* (New York: Simon & Schuster, 1982), p. 198.

14. Ibid., p. 197.

15. "Presidential Success on Votes 1953–1973," *Nixon: The Fifth Year of His Presidency* (Washington, D.C.: Congressional Quarterly, 1974), p. 58.

16. Gerald S. Strober and Deborah H. Strober, *Nixon: An Oral History of His Presidency* (New York: HarperCollins, 1992), p. 89.

17. "Ford's Political Record: Consistent Conservatism," *President Ford: The Man and His Record,* p. 27.

18. Fred P. Graham, "Ford Hints Move to

Oust Douglas," *New York Times,* November 8, 1969, p. 16.

19. Ibid., p. 1.

20. Marjorie Hunter, "Ford Concedes Aid of Justice Agency," *New York Times,* November 22, 1973, p. 42.

21. terHorst, *Gerald Ford and the Future of the Presidency,* p. 21.

22. Hunter, "Ford Concedes Aid of Justice Agency," p. 1.

23. John W. Finney, "The Mood Is Ugly, the Target Is Douglas," *New York Times,* April 19, 1970, p. 166.

24. Author interview with Gerald Ford, Rancho Mirage, Calif., March 23, 2003.

25. Richard Nixon to Gerald Ford, August 4, 1969, Gerald R. Ford Personal Papers, New York, N.Y.

4: THE WATERGATE BLUES

1. H. R. Haldeman, *The Haldeman Diaries: Inside the Nixon White House* (New York: G. P. Putnam's Sons, 1994), p. 208.

2. Theodore H. White, *The Making of the President 1972* (New York: Atheneum, 1973).

3. Ibid., pp. 49–50.

4. Lewis Chester, Call McCrystal, Stephen Aris, and William Shawcross, *Watergate:*

The Full Inside Circle (New York: Ballantine Books, 1973), p. 150.

5. Author interview with Gerald Ford, Rancho Mirage, Calif., March 23, 2003.

6. Strober and Strober, *Nixon: An Oral History of His Presidency,* p. 334.

7. *Watergate and the White House, Volume 1, June 1972–July 1973* (Washington, D.C.: Congressional Quarterly, 1973), p. 11.

8. Staff of the *New York Times, The White House Transcripts: Submission of Recorded Presidential Conversations to the Committee on the Judiciary of the House of Representatives by President Richard Nixon* (New York: Bantam Books, 1974), p. 823.

9. Robert B. Semple Jr., "2nd Campaign Tour Planned for Nixon," *New York Times,* September 20, 1972, p. 34.

10. Ford, *A Time to Heal,* p. 98.

11. Haldeman, *The Haldeman Diaries,* p. 504.

12. The President, Haldeman, and Dean, Oval Office. September 15, 1972 (5:27 to 6:17 p.m.), *Watergate: Chronology of a Crisis,* volume 2 (Washington, D.C.: Congressional Quarterly, 1974), pp. 382–83.

13. Clark R. Mollenhoff, *Game Plan for Disaster* (New York: W. W. Norton &

Company, 1976), p. 236.

14. terHorst, *Gerald Ford and the Future of the Presidency*, p. 136.

15. *Watergate and the White House, June 1972–July 1973*, p. 29.

16. Richard Matthew Pious, "Richard M. Nixon: The Resignation of Vice President Agnew," in Henry Graff, ed., *The Presidents: A Reference History*, second edition (New York: Charles Scribner's Sons, 1996), p. 529.

17. Lester A. Sobel, ed., *Presidential Succession: Ford, Rockefeller and the 25th Amendment* (New York: Facts on File, 1975), p. 40.

5: Changing of the Guard

1. John Adams, in a letter to his wife, Abigail Adams, December 19, 1793, Adams Papers, Massachusetts Historical Society, Boston, Massachusetts. Cited in David McCullough, *John Adams* (New York: Simon & Schuster, 2001), p. 447.

2. Gerald R. Ford, in televised remarks to the nation after his swearing-in as vice president of the United States by Chief Justice Warren E. Burger before a joint session of Congress in the U.S. Capitol, Washington, D.C., December 6, 1973.

3. terHorst, *Gerald Ford and the Future of the Presidency,* p. 168.

4. Seymour Hersh, "The Pardon: Nixon, Ford, Haig, and the Transfer of Power," *Atlantic Monthly,* August 1983.

5. terHorst, *Gerald Ford and the Future of the Presidency,* pp. 141–42.

6. Ibid., p. 158.

7. Ron Nessen, *It Sure Looks Different from the Inside* (Chicago: Playboy Press, 1978), p. 5.

8. Reeves, *A Ford, Not a Lincoln,* pp. 44–45.

9. *Watergate: Chronology of a Crisis,* volume 2, p. 204.

10. terHorst, *Gerald Ford and the Future of the Presidency,* pp. 176–77.

11. *Watergate and the White House, Volume 3, January–September 1974* (New York: Facts on File, 1974), p. 253.

12. Ibid.

13. Robert T. Hartmann, *Palace Politics: An Inside Account of the Ford Years* (New York: McGraw-Hill, 1980), p. 121.

14. Reeves, *A Ford, Not a Lincoln,* pp. 46, 49.

15. Strober and Strober, *Nixon: An Oral History of His Presidency,* p. 334.

16. terHorst, *Gerald Ford and the Future of the Presidency,* p. 168.

17. *President Ford: The Man and His Record* (Washington, D.C.: Congressional Quarterly, 1974), pp. 29, 65.

18. Frank Mankiewicz, *U.S. v. Richard M. Nixon: The Final Crisis* (New York: Quadrangle Books, 1975), p. 176.

19. *President Ford: The Man and His Record,* pp. 29, 62.

20. Clark R. Mollenhoff, *Game Plan for Disaster* (New York: W. W. Norton & Company, 1976), p. 349.

21. Reeves, *A Ford, Not a Lincoln,* pp. 11–12, 27–28.

22. Haldeman, *The Haldeman Diaries,* p. 288.

23. Bruce Oudes, ed., *From the President: Richard Nixon's Secret Files* (New York: Harper & Row, 1989), pp. 611–12.

24. Nixon, *RN,* p. 1057.

25. George Bush, *All the Best, George Bush: My Life in Letters and Other Writings* (New York: Scribner, 1999), pp. 186–87.

26. Nessen, *It Sure Looks Different from the Inside,* pp. 6–7.

27. Bush, *All the Best, George Bush,* p. 191.

28. Linda Amster, "Events Leading to the Resignation of Richard M. Nixon," in Staff of the *New York Times, The End of a Presidency* (New York: Holt, Rinehart and

Winston, 1974), p. 274.

29. terHorst, *Gerald Ford and the Future of the Presidency,* p. 185.
30. Thomas Jefferson, in a letter to Elbridge Gerry, May 13, 1797; cited in Gorton Carruth and Eugene Ehrlich, *American Quotations* (New York: Wings Books, 1992), p. 567.
31. Gerald R. Ford, in his inaugural address in the East Room of the White House, August 9, 1974.

6: THE PARDON MEETS WHIP INFLATION NOW

1. terHorst, *Gerald Ford and the Future of the Presidency,* p. 188.
2. "The Once and Future Ford," *Newsweek,* August 19, 1974, p. 23.
3. Walter Isaacson, *Kissinger: A Biography* (New York: Simon & Schuster, 1992), p. 601.
4. Author interview with Gerald Ford, Rancho Mirage, Calif., March 23, 2003.
5. Reeves, *A Ford, Not a Lincoln,* p. 150.
6. Bush, *All the Best, George Bush,* p. 192.
7. Reeves, *A Ford, Not a Lincoln,* p. 150.
8. Herbert S. Parmet, "Gerald R. Ford," in Graff, *The Presidents,* p. 537.
9. Author interview with Gerald Ford, Ran-

cho Mirage, Calif., March 23, 2003.

10. Reeves, *A Ford, Not a Lincoln,* p. 69.

11. Barry Werth, *31 Days: The Crisis That Gave Us the Government We Have Today* (New York: Nan A. Talese/Doubleday, 2006), pp. 220–21.

12. Bob Woodward, "Gerald R. Ford," in Caroline Kennedy, ed., *Profiles in Courage for Our Time* (New York: Hyperion, 2002), p. 294.

13. Jeff Jacoby, "An Award JFK Would Have Liked," *Boston Globe,* May 24, 2001, p. A23.

14. Werth, *31 Days,* p. 331.

15. terHorst, *Gerald Ford and the Future of the Presidency,* p. 238.

16. "Should Nixon Be Granted Immunity?" *Newsweek,* August 19, 1974, p. 17.

17. Hartmann, *Palace Politics,* p. 258.

18. Cannon, *Time and Chance,* p. 378.

19. Ibid., p. 380.

20. terHorst, *Gerald Ford and the Future of the Presidency,* p. 227.

21. Strober and Strober, *Nixon: An Oral History of His Presidency,* p. 486.

22. Parmet, "Gerald R. Ford," p. 537.

23. Nessen, *It Sure Looks Different from the Inside,* p. 33.

24. Gerald R. Ford, in a question-and-

answer session before the Northern Illinois Newspaper Association at the Chicago Airport Marriott Inn, March 12, 1976; the transcript appears in *The Presidential Campaign 1976, Volume Two, Part One: Gerald R. Ford,* pp. 248–49.

25. Reeves, *A Ford, Not a Lincoln,* pp. 113–14.
26. Werth, *31 Days,* p. 332.
27. Isaacson, *Kissinger,* p. 602.
28. Ford, *A Time to Heal,* p. 194.
29. Reeves, *A Ford, Not a Lincoln,* p. 160n.
30. Hartmann, *Palace Politics,* p. 298.
31. James Mann, *The Rise of the Vulcans* (New York: Viking, 2004), p. 59.
32. Seymour Hersh, "Huge CIA Operation Reported in U.S. Against Anti-War Forces," *New York Times,* December 22, 1974.
33. Timothy Naftali, *Blind Spot: The Secret History of American Terrorism* (New York: Basic Books, 2005), pp. 78–79.
34. A. Denis Clift, *With Presidents at the Summit* (Fairfax, Va.: George Mason University Press, 1993), pp. 81–103.

7: THE AGONY OF PEACE

1. Jacoby, "An Award JFK Would Have Liked," p. A23.

2. Werth, *31 Days,* p. 333.

3. Ibid., pp. 316–17.

4. Lou Cannon, *Governor Reagan: His Rise to Power* (New York: PublicAffairs, 2003), p. 194.

5. William Hyland, *Mortal Rivals: Superpower Relations from Nixon to Reagan* (New York: Random House, 1987), pp. 76–77.

6. Ford, *A Time to Heal,* p. 219.

7. Isaacson, *Kissinger,* pp. 627–28.

8. Ibid.

9. John Robert Greene, *The Presidency of Gerald R. Ford* (Lawrence, Kan.: University Press of Kansas, 1995), p. 68.

10. Nessen, *It Sure Looks Different from the Inside,* pp. 83–87.

11. David M. O'Brien, "Restoring the Rule of Law," in Bernard J. Firestone and Alexy Ugrinsky, eds., *Gerald R. Ford and the Politics of Post-Watergate America* (Westport, Conn.: Greenwood Press, 1993), p. 116.

12. Stephen Markman, quoted in ibid., p. 116.

13. Henry Kissinger, *Ending the Vietnam War* (New York: Simon & Schuster, 2003), p. 504.

14. Ford, *A Time to Heal,* p. 250.

15. Kissinger, *Ending the Vietnam War,* p. 507.

16. Hartmann, *Palace Politics,* pp. 318–19.

17. Jerrold L. Schecter, "The Final Days: The Political Struggles to End the Vietnam War," in Firestone and Ugrinsky, *Gerald R. Ford and the Politics of Post-Watergate America,* p. 541.

18. Oliver Todd, *Cruel April* (New York: W. W. Norton & Company, 1987), p. 60.

19. "A New Dunkirk in Indochina," *Newsweek,* April 17, 1975, p. 39.

20. Ford, *A Time to Heal,* p. 253.

21. Nguyen Van Thieu, in excerpts from his resignation speech as translated in "Two Views on Who's to Blame," *U.S. News and World Report,* May 5, 1975, p. 20.

22. Gerald R. Ford, remarks at Tulane University, New Orleans, April 23, 1975, as reported in "An Agenda for America's Third Century," *Department of State Bulletin,* May 12, 1975, p. 593.

23. Richard L. Madden, "Ford Says Indochina War Is Finished for America," *New York Times,* April 24, 1975, p. 73.

24. "Americans Oppose Arms for Saigon, Gallup Poll Shows," *New York Times,* April 24, 1975, p. 193.

25. Ford, remarks at Tulane University,

April 23, 1975, p. 593.

26. Ibid.

27. Henry Kissinger, *Years of Renewal* (New York: Simon & Schuster, 1999), p. 1064.

28. Kissinger, *Ending the Vietnam War,* pp. 535–36.

29. Isaacson, *Kissinger,* p. 645.

30. Hartmann, *Palace Politics,* p. 319.

31. Kenneth M. Quinn to Henry Kissinger, April 5, 1975, Gerald Ford Library and Museum, Ann Arbor, Mich.

32. Henry Kissinger to Graham Martin, April 17, 1975 (cable), Ford Library, Ann Arbor, Mich.

33. Henry Kissinger to Graham Martin, April 24, 1975 (cable), Ford Library, Ann Arbor, Mich.

34. Operation Frequent Wind (radio messages), April 29, 1975, Ford Library, Ann Arbor, Mich.

35. Author interview with Gerald Ford, Rancho Mirage, Calif., March 23, 2003.

36. Author interview with Fred Meijer, Grand Rapids, Mich., April 3, 2000.

37. Douglas Brinkley, "Of Ladders and Letters," *Time,* April 24, 2000.

8: The *Mayaguez* Incident and the Helsinki Accords

1. Richard M. Nixon, in a nationally televised address announcing U.S. incursions in Cambodia, April 30, 1970.
2. William Shawcross, *Side-Show: Kissinger, Nixon and the Destruction of Cambodia* (New York: Simon & Schuster, 1979), p. 432n.
3. Ford, *A Time to Heal,* p. 276.
4. "Comments of a Liberated Crew," *Time,* May 26, 1975, p. 17.
5. Kissinger, *Years of Renewal,* p. 551.
6. Nessen, *It Sure Looks Different from the Inside,* p. 122.
7. Ibid., pp. 125–26.
8. Shawcross, *Side-Show,* pp. 433n–34n.
9. Ford, *A Time to Heal,* p. 284.
10. Author interview with Richard Norton Smith, Washington, D.C., October 17, 2006.
11. Nessen, *It Sure Looks Different from the Inside,* p. 120.
12. Kissinger, *Years of Renewal,* p. 575.
13. Ford, *A Time to Heal,* p. 284.
14. Gerald R. Ford, in remarks announcing his candidacy for the Republican nomination for president at a ceremony in the White House Oval Office, July 8, 1975;

the transcript is in *The Presidential Campaign 1976, Volume Two, Part One: Gerald R. Ford,* pp. 1–2.

15. William Korey, *Human Rights and the Helsinki Accords* (New York: Foreign Policy Association, 1983), p. 7.

16. Aleksandr I. Solzhenitsyn, *The Gulag Archipelago* (New York: Harper & Row, 1973), p. 4.

17. Philip Shabecoff, "Ford Avoided Visit by Solzhenitsyn," *New York Times,* July 3, 1975, p. 5.

18. Ford, *A Time to Heal,* p. 298.

19. "Ford vs. Solzhenitsyn," *New York Times,* July 4, 1975, p. 22.

20. Joseph Kraft, "Solzhenitsyn's Message," *Washington Post,* July 3, 1975, p. A19.

21. Nessen, *It Sure Looks Different from the Inside,* p. 345.

22. Author interview with Gerald Ford, Rancho Mirage, Calif., March 23, 2003.

23. "Ford's Big Gamble on Détente," *Newsweek,* August 4, 1975, p. 16.

24. "European Security Conference Discussed by President Ford," *Department of State Bulletin,* volume 73, number 1885, August 11, 1975, pp. 204–6.

25. Author interview with Gerald Ford, Rancho Mirage, Calif., March 23, 2003.

26. Thomas J. Bray, "Gerald Rudolph Ford, Jr.," in James Taranto and Leonard Leo, eds., *Presidential Leadership: Rating the Best and the Worst in the White House* (New York: Wall Street Journal Books, 2004), p. 183.

27. Sand Vogelsang, "Diplomacy of Human Rights," *International Studies Quarterly,* volume 23, number 2, June 1979, pp. 222–23.

28. Henry E. Catto, Jr., *Ambassador at Sea: The High and Low Adventures of a Diplomat* (Austin, Tex.: University of Texas Press, 1998), p. 145.

29. Author interview with Gerald Ford, Rancho Mirage, Calif., March 23, 2003.

9: LOOKING FOR TRACTION

1. Nessen, *It Sure Looks Different from the Inside,* p. 78.

2. Author interview with Gerald Ford, Rancho Mirage, Calif., March 23, 2003.

3. Reeves, *A Ford, Not a Lincoln,* pp. 118, 201–2, 202n.

4. William A. Rusher, *The Rise of the Right* (New York: William Morrow & Company, 1984), p. 263.

5. Parmet, "Gerald R. Ford," p. 537.

6. Reeves, *A Ford, Not a Lincoln,* p. 147.

7. Author interview with Gerald Ford, Rancho Mirage, Calif., March 23, 2003.

8. Isaacson, *Kissinger,* pp. 630–35.

9. Ibid., p. 631

10. Ibid.

11. Author interview with Gerald Ford, Rancho Mirage, Calif., March 23, 2003.

12. Reeves, *A Ford, Not a Lincoln,* p. 153.

13. Nessen, *It Sure Looks Different from the Inside,* pp. 85, 88, 89.

14. Author interview with Gerald Ford, Rancho Mirage, Calif., March 23, 2003.

15. Ford, *A Time to Heal,* pp. 306–7.

16. "Betty Ford Gaffe," *National Review,* August 29, 1975, p. 922.

17. Reeves, *A Ford, Not a Lincoln,* p. 104.

18. Cannon, *Governor Reagan,* p. 402.

19. Nessen, *It Sure Looks Different from the Inside,* pp. 179–82.

20. "Ford's Brush with Death," *Newsweek,* September 15, 1975, p. 22.

21. Nessen, *It Sure Looks Different from the Inside,* pp. 183–85.

22. Ibid., p. 186.

23. "Assassination: An Endless Nightmare," *U.S. News & World Report,* October 6, 1975, p. 19.

24. Author interview with Gerald Ford, Rancho Mirage, Calif., March 23, 2003.

25. Ford, *A Time to Heal,* pp. 294–95.

26. Cannon, *Governor Reagan,* p. 402.
27. "What City Service Costs," *Newsweek,* August 4, 1975, p. 24.
28. Ford, *A Time to Heal,* p. 315.
29. Ibid.
30. Jason Berger, "Carey, Hugh L(eo)," in Eleanora W. Schoenebaum, ed., *Profiles of an Era: The Nixon/Ford Years* (New York: Harcourt Brace Jovanovich, 1979), p. 113.
31. "New York's Last Gasp?" *Newsweek,* August 4, 1975, p. 18.
32. Ford, *A Time to Heal,* p. 316.
33. Hartmann, *Palace Politics,* p. 357.
34. *A Time to Heal,* p. 318.
35. Ibid., p. 328.
36. Nessen, *It Sure Looks Different from the Inside,* p. 158.
37. Ford, *A Time to Heal,* p. 328.
38. John D'Emilio, "Beame, Abraham D(avid)," in Schoenebaum, *Profiles of an Era,* p. 39.
39. Ford, *A Time to Heal,* pp. 318–19.
40. "Ford to City: Drop Dead," *Daily News* (New York), October 30, 1975, p. 1.
41. Gerald R. Ford, in comments at a White House question-and-answer session with twenty-three reporters in the Oval Office, December 31, 1975; the transcript appears in *The Presidential Campaign 1976,*

Volume Two, Part One: Gerald R. Ford, p. 48.

42. D'Emilio, "Beame, Abraham D(avid)," p. 39.

43. Gerald R. Ford, in comments at a campaign session with local officials in Louisiana at Hanger Auditorium, Barksdale Air Force Base, Bossier City, Louisiana, April 27, 1976; the transcript appears in *The Presidential Campaign 1976, Volume Two, Part One: Gerald R. Ford,* p. 383.

44. Nessen, *It Sure Looks Different from the Inside,* pp. 155–56, 159–60.

45. Author interview with Gerald Ford, Rancho Mirage, Calif., March 23, 2003.

46. Ibid.

47. Nessen, *It Sure Looks Different from the Inside,* pp. 159–60.

48. "Scenario of the Shake-up," *Time,* November 17, 1975, p. 19.

49. Nessen, *It Sure Looks Different from the Inside,* p. 249.

50. Christopher Hitchens, *The Trial of Henry Kissinger* (New York: Verso, 2001), pp. 90–107.

51. Author interview with Gerald Ford, Rancho Mirage, Calif., March 23, 2003.

52. Hitchens, *The Trial of Henry Kissinger,* p. 99.

53. Author interview with Gerald Ford, Rancho Mirage, Calif., March 23, 2003.

10: THE BICENTENNIAL CAMPAIGN

1. " 'It Looks Like Humphrey,' " *U.S. News & World Report,* November 17, 1975, p. 24.
2. "Gerald Ford's Improving Prospects," *Time,* June 23, 1975, p. 28.
3. Kevin P. Phillips, *The Emerging Republican Majority* (New Rochelle, N.Y.: Arlington House, 1969), p. 470.
4. James A. Baker III, in comments to anchor Tom Brokaw during NBC News's live coverage of Ronald Reagan's state funeral procession to the U.S. Capitol, June 9, 2004, 7:23 p.m. Eastern Daylight Time.
5. James A. Baker III, *"Work Hard, Study . . . And Keep Out of Politics!": Adventures from an Unexpected Public Life* (New York: Putnam, 2006), pp. 44–45.
6. Nessen, *It Sure Looks Different from the Inside,* pp. 170–72.
7. Cited in ibid., pp. 190–91.
8. Lyndon B. Johnson, comment attributed in Carruth and Ehrlich, *American Quotations,* p. 470.
9. Lyndon B. Johnson, comment attributed

in Reeves, *A Ford, Not a Lincoln,* p. 25n.

10. "The Ridicule Problem," *Time,* January 5, 1976, p. 33.

11. Martin Schramm, *Running for President: A Journal of the Carter Campaign* (New York: Stein and Day, 1977), pp. 178–79.

12. Nessen, *It Sure Looks Different from the Inside,* pp. 172–75.

13. Author interview with Gerald Ford, Rancho Mirage, Calif., March 23, 2003.

14. Baker, *"Work Hard, Study . . . And Keep Out of Politics!"* p. 44.

15. Gerald R. Ford, *Humor and the Presidency* (New York: Arbor House, 1987), front jacket flap.

16. Ibid., pp. 48–49.

17. Ronald Reagan, quoted in Nessen, *It Sure Looks Different from the Inside,* p. 206.

18. Cannon, *Governor Reagan,* p. 424.

19. Richard B. Cheney, quoted in Ford, *Humor and the Presidency,* pp. 150–51.

20. Remarks of Gerald R. Ford in Philadelphia, July 4, 1976, Gerald R. Ford Library and Museum, Grand Rapids, Mich.

21. Author interview with Robert Hartmann, Bethesda, Md., November 11, 2006.

22. Richard B. Cheney, quoted in Nessen, *It Sure Looks Different from the Inside,* p. 230.

23. Gerald R. Ford, in remarks accepting the nomination for president at the Republican National Convention, Kemper Arena, Kansas City, August 19, 1976; the transcript appears in *The Presidential Campaign 1976, Volume Two, Part Two: Gerald R. Ford,* pp. 693–99.

24. James J. Kilpatrick, "Will the Republican Party Survive Kansas City?" *National Review,* September 16, 1976, p. 1004.

25. Author interview with Gerald Ford, Rancho Mirage, Calif., March 23, 2003.

26. Nessen, *It Sure Looks Different from the Inside,* p. 239.

27. Nelson A. Rockefeller, in remarks at the joint press conference announcing President Gerald R. Ford's selection of Senator Robert J. Dole as his vice presidential running mate, Kansas City, August 19, 1976; the transcript appears in *The Presidential Campaign 1976, Volume Two, Part Two: Gerald R. Ford,* p. 692.

28. George Bush, in a letter to John Fonteno of Houston, Tex., August 17, 1976, in Bush, *All the Best, George Bush,* p. 261.

29. Richard Nixon to Gerald Ford, April 22, 1976, Gerald R. Ford Personal Papers, New York, N.Y.

30. Richard Nixon to Gerald Ford, Febru-

ary 12, 1976, Gerald R. Ford Personal Papers, New York, N.Y.

31. Richard Nixon to Gerald Ford, August 20, 1976, Gerald R. Ford Personal Papers, New York, N.Y.

32. Author interview with Richard Norton Smith, Washington, D.C., October 17, 2006.

33. Nessen, *It Sure Looks Different from the Inside,* p. 250.

34. Ibid., pp. 263–67.

35. Ford, *A Time to Heal,* p. 422.

36. Ibid., pp. 422–23.

37. William F. Buckley Jr., quoted in Parmet, "Gerald R. Ford," p. 549.

38. Nessen, *It Sure Looks Different from the Inside,* p. 278.

39. Ford, *A Time to Heal,* pp. 431–32; also Nessen, *It Sure Looks Different from the Inside,* p. 310.

40. Nessen, *It Sure Looks Different from the Inside,* p. 316.

41. Ibid., p. 319.

42. Cited in ibid., p. 320.

43. Ford, *A Time to Heal,* p. 437.

44. Billy Graham to Gerald Ford, November 24, 1976, Gerald R. Ford Personal Papers, New York, N.Y.

45. Gerald Ford, State of the Union ad-

dress, January 12, 1977.

46. Mark Updegrove, *Second Acts* (Guilford, Conn.: Lyons Press, 2006), p. 114.

47. Kissinger, *Years of Renewal,* p. 1066.

48. Ibid., p. 40.

49. Author interview with Richard Norton Smith, Washington, D.C., October 17, 2006.

50. Ben Bradlee, *A Good Life: Newspapering and Other Adventures* (New York: Simon & Schuster, 1995), p. 408.

51. Billy Graham to Gerald Ford, November 24, 1976, Gerald R. Ford Personal Papers, New York, N.Y.

52. Cited in Nessen, *It Sure Looks Different from the Inside,* p. 320.

11: RETIREMENT DECADES

1. Richard Nixon to Gerald Ford, January 3, 1977, Gerald R. Ford Personal Papers, New York, N.Y.

2. Richard Nixon to Gerald Ford, May 14, 1978, Gerald R. Ford Personal Papers, New York, N.Y.

3. Author interview with Gerald Ford, Rancho Mirage, Calif., March 23, 2003.

4. Martin Schram, "Ford Says He Won't Be

a Candidate," *Washington Post,* March 16, 1980.

5. Updegrove, *Second Acts,* p. 129.
6. Author interview with Gerald Ford, Rancho Mirage, Calif., March 23, 2003.
7. Ford, *A Time to Heal,* pp. 289–90.
8. Author interview with Gerald Ford, Rancho Mirage, Calif., March 23, 2003.
9. Douglas Brinkley, *The Unfinished Presidency: Jimmy Carter's Journey Beyond the White House* (New York: Viking, 1998), pp. 68–69.
10. Author interview with Gerald Ford, Rancho Mirage, Calif., March 23, 2003.
11. Betty Ford, *A Glad Awakening* (New York: Doubleday, 1987), pp. 1–10, 265.
12. Updegrove, *Second Acts,* p. 121.
13. Ibid.
14. Ibid., pp. 113–14.
15. Richard Reeves, "I'm Sorry, Mr. President," *American Heritage,* December 1996.
16. Author interview with Gerald Ford, Rancho Mirage, Calif., March 23, 2003.
17. Bob Woodward, "Gerald R. Ford," pp. 293–315.
18. Author interview with Gerald Ford, Rancho Mirage, Calif., March 23, 2003.
19. Gerald R. Ford, "The Path Back to Dignity," *New York Times,* October 4, 1998.

20. Richard L. Berke, "The Testing of a President: An Overview," *New York Times,* October 4, 1998.

21. Gerald Ford and Jimmy Carter, "A Time to Heal Our Nation," *New York Times,* December 21, 1998.

22. Author interview with Gerald Ford, Rancho Mirage, Calif., March 23, 2003.

23. Remarks of Senator Edward Kennedy, Presentation of the 2001 Profile in Courage Award to President Gerald Ford, JFK Library and Museum, Boston, Massachusetts, May 21, 2001.

24. Caroline Kennedy to Gerald Ford, April 30, 2001, Gerald R. Ford Personal Papers, New York, N.Y.

25. Theodore Hesburgh to Gerald Ford, May 30, 2001, Gerald R. Ford Personal Papers, New York, N.Y.

26. Lord Callaghan to Gerald Ford, June 12, 2001, Gerald R. Ford Personal Papers, New York, N.Y.

27. Author interview with Gerald Ford, Rancho Mirage, Calif., March 23, 2003.

28. David Hume Kennerly, "Becoming the President," *New York Times,* December 28, 2006.

29. "Gerald R. Ford," editorial, *New York Times,* December 28, 2006.

MILESTONES

1913   Born on July 14 as
Leslie Lynch
King Jr., in
Omaha,
Nebraska; his
mother, Dorothy
Gardner King,
flees her
marriage two
weeks later and
takes him to live
with her family
in Grand Rapids,
Michigan

1917	Dorothy King marries a Grand Rapids businessman named Gerald R. Ford; he informally adopts her son, who is hereafter known as Gerald R. Ford Jr.
1931–35	Attends the University of Michigan; plays center and linebacker on the football team and is named Most Valuable Player of the 1934 team
1935	Graduates from the University of Michigan
	Receives offers from the Green Bay Packers and the Detroit Lions to play professional football

	Becomes a boxing coach and an assistant football coach at Yale University
	Legally changes name to Gerald R. Ford Jr.
1938–41	Attends Yale Law School
1940	Volunteers for Wendell Willkie's presidential campaign and attends first Republican National Convention
1941	Graduates in the top third of his law school class at Yale; returns to Grand Rapids to practice law and becomes active in local politics

1942–45	Serves in the U.S. Navy during World War II and sees action in the Pacific aboard the USS *Monterey*
1946	Receives honorable discharge from the navy and returns to Grand Rapids, resuming his involvement in reforming local politics
1948	Successfully challenges Representative Bartel J. Jonkman in the Republican congressional primary
	Marries Elizabeth Ann Bloomer Warren
	Elected to U.S. Congress

1949	Begins first term in Congress and meets and befriends fellow representative Richard Nixon
1950	Appointed to the House Appropriations Committee
1952	Dwight Eisenhower elected president; Republicans take control of Congress
1954	Democrats regain control of Congress in midterm elections
1959	Joins movement within the House Republican caucus to replace House Minority Leader Joseph Martin with Charles Halleck

1960	Mentioned as possible Republican vice presidential nominee but is not chosen
	John F. Kennedy elected president, defeating Richard Nixon
1963	Elected House Republican Conference chairman
	President Kennedy assassinated in Dallas
	Appointed by President Lyndon B. Johnson to serve on the Warren Commission to investigate Kennedy's death

1964	Warren Commission issues its report, concluding that there was no evidence of a conspiracy in Kennedy's assassination
	Decides to challenge Halleck for the post of House minority leader
1965	Elected House minority leader by a 73–67 vote
	Publishes (with Jack Stiles) *Portrait of the Assassin*
1966	Congressional Republicans make strong gains in the midterm elections
1968	Again mentioned as possible Republican vice presidential nominee

	Richard Nixon elected president
1969	Unsuccessfully calls for the impeachment and removal from office of Justice William O. Douglas, on ethics grounds
1972	Watergate break-in
	Nixon reelected president
1973	Vice President Spiro Agnew resigns on October 10 after pleading no contest to bribery and tax evasion charges
	Nominated by President Nixon on October 12 to be vice president
	Confirmed by Congress as vice president and sworn in on December 6

1974	Supreme Court orders Nixon to turn over White House tapes related to Watergate
	House Judiciary Committee approves three articles of impeachment against Nixon
	Nixon announces his resignation on August 8, effective the next day
	Sworn in as the thirty-eighth president of the United States on August 9
	Announces support for clemency for Vietnam War draft evaders
	Nominates Nelson Rockefeller to be vice president

Pardons Nixon on September 8 for any crimes he may have committed as president

Announces "Whip Inflation Now" program

Meets with Soviet leader Leonid Brezhnev in Vladivostok

1975   Announces on April 23 that the Vietnam War "is finished as far as America is concerned."

Orders the emergency evacuation of American personnel and South Vietnamese refugees

The South Vietnamese capital of Saigon falls on April 30

Cambodia seizes the *Mayaguez,* a U.S. merchant ship; marines sent in to rescue the crew

Travels to Helsinki to meet with the leaders of thirty-four other nations to sign the Final Act of the Conference on Security and Cooperation in Europe

Survives two assassination attempts in California, one by Lynette "Squeaky" Fromme and one by Sara Jane Moore

Refuses to support
a federal bailout
for New York
City but later
approves a line of
credit once city
and state leaders
take steps to
address the crisis

Reorganizes
cabinet, naming
Donald
Rumsfeld as
secretary of
defense, Elliot
Richardson as
secretary of
commerce,
George H. W.
Bush as director
of CIA, Dick
Cheney as White
House chief of
staff, and Brent
Scowcroft as
national security
adviser

	Urges Rockefeller to withdraw his name from consideration as the 1976 vice presidential nominee
	Nominates John Paul Stevens to the U.S. Supreme Court
1976	Celebration of the U.S. bicentennial
	Defeats Ronald Reagan for the Republican presidential nomination; selects Senator Robert Dole as his running mate
	Debates Democratic nominee Jimmy Carter three times
	Loses presidential election to Carter
1977	Leaves office on January 20

1979	Publishes his memoir, *A Time to Heal*
1980	Discusses the possibility of joining Reagan's ticket as the vice presidential candidate, but no agreement is struck
1981	Attends funeral of Egyptian president Anwar Sadat
1982	The Betty Ford Center opens
1987	Publishes *Humor and the Presidency*
1998	Urges "rebuke" and "censure" as alternatives to an impeachment trial in the case of President Bill Clinton

1999	Receives the Presidential Medal of Freedom and the Congressional Gold Medal
2001	Receives the Profile in Courage Award from the John F. Kennedy Foundation
2006	Dies on December 26, having surpassed Ronald Reagan as the nation's longest-lived president

SELECTED BIBLIOGRAPHY

Baker, James A. III. *"Work Hard, Study . . . And Keep Out of Politics!": Adventures from an Unexpected Public Life.* New York: Putnam, 2006.

Bolling, Richard. *Power in the House.* New York: Capricorn Books, 1968.

Bradlee, Ben. *A Good Life: Newspapering and Other Adventures.* New York: Simon & Schuster, 1995.

Brinkley, Douglas. "Of Ladders and Letters," *Time,* April 24, 2000.

———. *The Unfinished Presidency: Jimmy Carter's Journey Beyond the White House.* New York: Viking, 1998.

Bush, George. *All the Best, George Bush: My Life in Letters and Other Writings.* New York: Scribner, 1999.

Cannon, James. *Time and Chance: Gerald Ford's Appointment with History: 1913–1974.* New York: HarperCollins, 1994.

Cannon, Lou. *Governor Reagan: His Rise to Power.* New York: PublicAffairs, 2003.

Carruth, Gorton, and Eugene Ehrlich. *American Quotations.* New York: Wings Books, 1992.

Catto, Henry E., Jr. *Ambassador at Sea: The High and Low Adventures of a Diplomat.* Austin: University of Texas Press, 1998.

Chester, Lewis, Call McCrystal, Stephen Aris, and William Shawcross. *Watergate: The Full Inside Circle.* New York: Ballantine Books, 1973.

Ehrlichman, John D. *Witness to Power.* New York: Simon & Schuster, 1982.

Firestone, Bernard J., and Alexy Ugrinsky (eds.). *Gerald R. Ford and the Politics of Post-Watergate America.* Westport, Conn.: Greenwood Press, 1993.

Ford, Gerald R. *Humor and the Presidency.* New York: Arbor House, 1987.

———. *A Time to Heal.* New York: Harper & Row, 1979.

———. "What Can Save the G.O.P.?" *Fortune,* January 1965, p. 110.

———. and John R. Stiles, *Portrait of the Assassin.* New York: Simon & Schuster, 1965.

Gergen, David. *Eyewitness to Power.* New York: Simon & Schuster, 2000.

Graff, Henry F. (ed.). *The Presidents: A Reference History,* second edition. New York: Charles Scribner's Sons, 1996.

Greene, John Robert. *The Presidency of Gerald R. Ford.* Lawrence: University Press of Kansas, 1995.

Haldeman, H. R. *The Haldeman Diaries: Inside the Nixon White House.* New York: G. P. Putnam's Sons, 1994.

Hartmann, Robert T. *Palace Politics: An Inside Account of the Ford Years.* New York: McGraw-Hill, 1980.

Hersh, Seymour. "The Pardon: Nixon, Ford, Haig, and the Transfer of Power," *Atlantic Monthly,* August 1983.

Hitchens, Christopher. *The Trial of Henry Kissinger.* New York: Verso, 2001.

Horrocks, David A., and William H. McNitt. *Guide to Historical Materials in the Gerald R. Ford Library.* Ann Arbor, Mich.: Gerald R. Ford Library, 2003.

Kennedy, Caroline Kennedy (ed.). *Profiles in Courage for Our Time.* New York: Hyperion, 2002.

Kilpatrick, James J. "Will the Republican Party Survive Kansas City?" *National Review,* September 16, 1976.

Kingdon, John W. *Congressmen's Voting Decisions.* New York: Harper & Row, 1981.

Kissinger, Henry. *Ending the Vietnam War.* New York: Simon & Schuster, 2003.

———. *Years of Renewal.* New York: Simon & Schuster, 1999.

Knappman, Edward W., and Mary Elizabeth Clifford et al. (eds.). *Watergate and the White House.* New York: Facts on File, 1973–74.

Korey, William. *Human Rights and the Helsinki Accords.* New York: Foreign Policy Association, 1983.

Lukas, J. Anthony. *Nightmare: The Underside of the Nixon Years.* New York: Viking Press, 1976.

Mankiewicz, Frank. *U.S. v. Richard M. Nixon: The Final Crisis.* New York: Quadrangle Books, 1975.

Mann, James. *The Rise of the Vulcans.* New York: Viking, 2004.

Martin, Joseph W., with Charles Donovan. *My First Fifty Years in Politics.* New York: McGraw-Hill, 1960.

McCullough, David. *John Adams.* New York: Simon & Schuster, 2001.

Mollenhoff, Clark R. *Game Plan for Disaster.* New York: W. W. Norton & Company, 1976.

Nessen, Ron. *It Sure Looks Different from the Inside.* Chicago: Playboy Press, 1978.

The New York Times, Staff of. *The End of a Presidency.* New York: Holt, Rinehart and Winston, 1974.

————. *The White House Transcripts: Submission of Recorded Presidential Conversations to the Committee on the Judiciary of the House of Representatives by President Richard Nixon.* New York: Bantam Books, 1974.

Nixon, Richard M. *RN: The Memoirs of Richard Nixon.* New York: Grosset & Dunlap, 1978.

Nixon: The Fifth Year of His Presidency. Washington, D.C.: Congressional Quarterly, 1974.

Oudes, Bruce (ed.). *From the President: Richard Nixon's Secret Files.* New York: Harper & Row, 1989.

Peabody, Robert L. *The Ford-Halleck Minority Leadership Contest, 1965.* New York: McGraw-Hill, 1966.

Phillips, Kevin P. *The Emerging Republican Majority.* New Rochelle, N.Y.: Arlington House, 1969.

President Ford: The Man and His Record. Washington, D.C.: Congressional Quarterly, 1974.

The Presidential Campaign 1976, Volume Two, Part Two: Gerald R. Ford. Washington,

D.C.: U.S. Government Printing Office, 1979.

Reeves, Richard. *A Ford, Not a Lincoln.* New York: Harcourt Brace Jovanovich, 1975.

Ripley, Randall B. *Party Leaders in the House of Representatives.* Washington, D.C.: Brookings Institution Press, 1967.

Rusher, William A. *The Rise of the Right.* New York: William Morrow & Company, 1984.

Schoenebaum, Eleanora W. (ed.). *Profiles of an Era: The Nixon/Ford Years.* New York: Harcourt Brace Jovanovich, 1979.

Schram, Martin. *Running for President: A Journal of the Carter Campaign.* New York: Stein and Day, 1977.

Shawcross, William. *Side-Show: Kissinger, Nixon and the Destruction of Cambodia.* New York: Simon & Schuster, 1979.

Sobel, Lester A. (ed.). *Presidential Succession: Ford, Rockefeller and the 25th Amendment.* New York: Facts on File, 1975.

Street, Julian. *Abroad at Home.* New York: Century, 1916.

Strober, Gerald S., and Deborah H. Strober. *Nixon: An Oral History of His Presidency.* New York: HarperCollins, 1992.

Tacheron, Donald, and Morris Udall. *The Job of the Congressman.* Indianapolis:

Bobbs-Merrill, 1970.

Taranto, James, and Leonard Leo (eds.). *Presidential Leadership: Rating the Best and the Worst in the White House.* New York: Wall Street Journal Books, 2004.

terHorst, Jerald F. *Gerald Ford and the Future of the Presidency.* New York: Third Press, 1974.

Tillett, Paul (ed.). *Inside Politics: The National Conventions, 1960.* New Brunswick, N.J.: Rutgers University Press, 1962.

Todd, Oliver. *Cruel April.* New York: W. W. Norton & Company, 1987.

Updegrove, Mark. *Second Acts.* Guilford, Conn.: Lyons Press, 2006.

Vestal, Bud. *Jerry Ford, Up Close: An Investigative Biography.* New York: Coward, McCann & Geoghegan, 1974.

Vogelsang, Sandy. "Diplomacy of Human Rights," *International Studies Quarterly,* volume 23, number 2, June 1979.

Wallechinsky, David. *David Wallechinksy's Twentieth Century: History with the Boring Parts Left Out.* New York: Little, Brown and Company, 1995.

The Warren Report. New York: The Associated Press, 1964.

Watergate and the White House, June 1972–July 1973. Washington, D.C.: Congressional Quarterly, 1973.

Watergate: Chronology of a Crisis, Volume 2. Washington, D.C.: Congressional Quarterly, 1974.

Wetterhahn, Ralph. *The Last Battle: The* Mayaguez *Incident and the End of the Vietnam War.* New York: Carroll & Graf, 2001.

White, Theodore H. *The Making of the President 1972.* New York: Atheneum, 1973.

ACKNOWLEDGMENTS

A few years ago, the historian Arthur Schlesinger Jr. asked me to write a book about Gerald R. Ford for his American Presidents Series. I've learned never to tell Arthur no; it's one of my smarter habits. Before long, I found myself holed up at the Ford Presidential Archive in Ann Arbor, poring over recently declassified documents pertaining to the fall of Saigon in 1975. To my surprise, Ford, against virtually all of his foreign policy gurus' advice, insisted that we evacuate as many South Vietnamese as possible. To celebrate the twenty-fifth anniversary of the end of the Vietnam War in 2000, I wrote a long essay for *Time* titled "Of Ladders and Letters," showcasing the new batch of documents. I used material from that *Time* article in this book.

Even though the Ford Library documents were illuminating on U.S. foreign policy from 1974 to 1977, they lacked emotive quality. I wondered where Ford's personal correspondence was located, letters that he had received from Barry Goldwater or Henry Kissinger or Billy Graham over the years. The hunt eventually led me to Glenn Horowitz Booksellers in Manhattan. In July 2006, Ford sold his personal library, correspondence, and mementos to Horowitz, the best manuscripts/archive dealer in America. It's a stunning collection.

Although the archive is closed from public viewing, that is until they find the proper institutional home, I was given special access. Here, at last, was the personal side of Ford I so desperately needed for my book. Whether it's Ford calling Madeleine Albright the "Tiger Woods of foreign policy" or lobbying behind the scenes so the folksinger Burl Ives could receive the Presidential Medal of Freedom or kibbitzing with Bess Truman on Jimmy Carter's flakiness, the collection sheds important new light on Ford's seminal place in twentieth-century American history, including his role on the Warren Commission, Watergate, the *Mayaguez* incident, the Helsinki Accords, and the end of the Vietnam War. But clearly the most extraordinary materials are original handwritten letters that Richard M. Nixon sent Ford from 1956 to 1994, which I quote throughout the narrative.

Besides bringing new Vietnam War and Nixon-Ford relationship evidence to light, I was granted a no-holds-barred interview with President Ford at his office in Rancho Mirage, California. (I had previously, for other projects, interviewed him in April 1998 and April 2000.) As always, his forthrightness was refreshing for a career politician.

In Rancho Mirage, his blue eyes had a slightly glazed, watery look, as if suffering from hay fever. Despite his age, however, Ford's broad shoulders weren't sloped, there was no loose unwrinkled skin hanging on his neck. "I had a close one," Ford explained of his latest stroke. "I was about as close to a collapse without literally falling as possible. Complete dizziness. The secret service and the person I was playing with saved me from falling. My blood pressure was very abnormal."

Throughout the process of writing this book I received editorial assistance from Shelby Sadler (research/line-editing), Andrew Travers (manuscript preparation), and Paul Golob (shepherding). Dr. Elaine K. Didier, director of the Ford Presidential Library and Museum in both Ann Arbor and Grand Rapids, constantly encouraged me in numerous ways. She is superb. Archivist David Horrocks of the Ford Presidential Library dutifully answered a barrage of queries. CBS News had me serve as the presidential historian for Gerald Ford's funeral and provided generous support of this project. And President Ford's longtime assistant Penny Circle was my Rock of Gibraltar throughout the three years it took me to finish.

ABOUT THE AUTHOR AND EDITOR

Douglas Brinkley is the director of the Theodore Roosevelt Center and professor of history at Tulane University. He is the author of biographies of Henry Ford, Jimmy Carter, Dean Acheson, James Forrestal, John Kerry, and Rosa Parks, and his most recent books include *The Great Deluge, The Boys of Pointe du Hoc,* and *Tour of Duty.* He is a contributing editor for *Vanity Fair,* the *Los Angeles Times Book Review,* and *American Heritage* and a frequent contributor to *The New York Times, The New Yorker,* and *The Atlantic Monthly.* He lives in New Orleans with his wife and children.

Arthur M. Schlesinger, Jr., is the pre-eminent political historian of our time. The recipient of two Pulitzer Prizes and a National Humanities Medal, he published the first volume of his autobiography, *A Life in the Twentieth Century,* in 2000.

The employees of Thorndike Press hope you have enjoyed this Large Print book. All our Thorndike and Wheeler Large Print titles are designed for easy reading, and all our books are made to last. Other Thorndike Press Large Print books are available at your library, through selected bookstores, or directly from us.

For information about titles, please call:
(800) 223-1244

or visit our Web site at:
www.gale.com/thorndike
www.gale.com/wheeler

To share your comments, please write:
Publisher
Thorndike Press
295 Kennedy Memorial Drive
Waterville, ME 04901